Christopher Smart's Verse Translation of Horace's *Odes*: Text and Introduction

edited by ARTHUR SHERBO

EDITIONS

ELS Editions
Department of English
University of Victoria
Victoria, BC
Canada V8W 3W1
www.elseditions.com

Founding Editor: Samuel L. Macey

General Editor: Luke Carson

Printed by CreateSpace

English literary studies monograph series
ISSN 0829-7681 ; 17
ISBN-10 0-920604-32-3
ISBN-13 978-0-920604-32-8

CONTENTS

Note on Production

Keyboarding, copy editing, and proofreading of the text of this volume were done by James Howald, Andrew Platt, and Gregory Van Houten of the Department of English of the University of Southern California, under the supervision of Robert Dilligan and Donald Greene, in the course of an experimental program for training graduate students in computer-assisted methods of scholarly book production. A system of bibliographic transcription and a computer editing program developed by Professor Dilligan were used. Photocomposition was done by Professor Dilligan at the Center for Computer Assisted Textual Analysis Project, University of California, San Diego, through the cooperation of its Coordinator, Michael Holzman. Financial support for this part of the production of the volume was provided by the Leo S. Bing Fund of the Department of English, University of Southern California.

INTRODUCTION

I.

Horace's influence on the writers and readers of the literature of the first three quarters of the eighteenth century was stronger and more pervasive than that of any other classical poet. One of the landmarks in English scholarship, Richard Bentley's edition of Horace published in 1711, came into being, Bentley tells us in his Preface, because he wanted to edit "some writer of the pleasanter sort. . . . My choice was HORACE, . . . because he, above all the ancients—thanks to his merit, or to a peculiar genius and gift for pleasing—was familiar to men's hands and hearts."[1] The inclusion of Horace's poetry in the curriculum of most English schools is well known, as is the fact that schoolboys not only had to translate from his work but also wrote imitations of his lyrics. Evidence that this early exposure to Horace's poetry had a lasting effect abounds, not least in the many voluntary and deliberate imitations of his poems, in the many published translations of parts or all of the canon, in the numerous allusions to him in eighteenth- century writing of all kinds, in the scholarly activity that focused upon his work, and in the continuous and impressive sale of his poetry, both in the original Latin and in translation.[2]

While we shall never be able to gauge precisely the influence of even one of Horace's works on eighteenth-century writers, his *Art of Poetry* was surely one of the more important critical documents of the age. The authors of the *Spectator* essays appended no fewer than fifty-four mottoes from it to their papers, and Pope paid handsome tribute to it in the *Essay on Criticism* (ll.653-56). But it was by no means only the writers, amateurs or professional men of letters, who recalled their Horace for an apposite quotation or allusion in one of their works; educated men in the professions, in the arts, in government, and, indeed, virtually everywhere, were ready to supply or recognize a line from the Latin poet. One could encounter a volume of Horace almost anywhere. Young Mat Prior, for example, was seen by the Earl of Dorset reading Horace in the tavern in which he was employed and thereby gained a university education at that generous nobleman's expense. And Tobias Smollett's Roderick Random set out for London with various necessary articles and "a small edition of Horace" (I.vii). But perhaps the greatest praise should go to the the gentleman of whom Lord Chesterfield wrote to his son in 1747 that he was "so good a manager of his time that he would not even lose that small portion of it which the calls of nature obliged to pass in the necessary house . . . . He bought a common edition of Horace, of which he tore off gradually a couple of pages, carried them with him to that necessary place, read them first and then sent them down as a sacrifice to Cloacina."[3]

Horace was much more, however, than a poet whose works were read, imitated, translated, and quoted; his life—or at least what was revealed of it by the presumably autobiographical parts of his poetry— served as a model for well-to-do amateurs of life and letters to emulate. Especially attractive to these admirers of Horace was the ideal—or idyl—of rustic, or semirustic, retirement.[4] The Latin poet's Sabine farm, by no means an unpretentious piece of real estate, was consciously and prominently in the mind of more than one English gentleman who, having one foot in London, set himself up in a country villa as well. Close enough to his base of operations, he was still sufficiently surrounded by the appurtenances of rusticity to preserve the image of retirement. And this gentleman, not content merely to emulate Horace in his physical removal from the city, strove manfully to pattern his life on the *modus vivendi* he could reconstruct from Horace's poetry. One further refinement remained: having retired to the country and having modelled his life on Horace's (most of the details of which he would have got from the sixth Satire of the second Book), he was now ready to write poems about his rustic existence—just as Horace had before him. John Pomfret's poem *The Choice*, which frequently turns up in anthologies, owes its continued appearance to the completeness with which, precisely in 1699, it handed over to the new century a poetic catalogue of the ideals of the Horatian way of life. Samuel Johnson included a six-paragraph account of Pomfret and his poetry in his *Lives* of the poets; late in the century he could write that "perhaps no composition in our language has oftener been perused than Pomfret's *Choice*." But far greater poets than Pomfret "retired," either in fact or in fiction; Alexander Pope, after all, also had his villa.

Usually, when one thinks of Pope and his contemporaries as modelling themselves upon and imitating Latin authors, particularly those of Augustus's reign, one accepts the convenient terms "Augustan" or "neo-classical" as applying to them and their age solely on that basis. Actually, in Reuben A. Brower's opinion, Horace and Pope lived in countries and at times when what was true of the earlier period was almost equally true of the later. Professor Brower quotes a few lines of a letter from Thomas Burnet to George Duckett of 1 June 1716, "I am now at my leisure hours reading Horace with some diligence and find the world was just the same then, that it continues to be now," and then comments:

> Though Thomas Burnet was historically naive in finding the
> world of Horace "just the same" as the Age of Anne, he could

easily have produced reasons to justify his impression. For example, he might have pointed out the broad historical parallels of the kind we have noted in speaking of *Windsor Forest*—between two societies in an era of concentration following an era of revolution, between nations just becoming aware of their imperial role, and between cultures enriched by increased leisure and easier contacts with "earth's distant ends." For the eighteenth-century gentleman enjoying the private benefits of these public improvements the world of Horace's *Satires* and *Epistles* offered striking parallels to his own. Like Horace, he could look about him and see some lives charmingly balanced between city and country, action and retirement, and other lives grossly submerged in political ambition or newly acquired wealth and conspicuous consumption. Whatever may have been the actualities of English life in the reign of Anne, it was quite easy for a citizen of that world to see himself and his fellows through Horace's eyes. We need to remember, of course, that Horace's world is not a documentary study of the Age of Augustus, but a poet's vision of reality. The fantasies of a Roman dinner party as pictured by Horace and the air of serenity that lingers about the Sabine farm are not Nature still, but Nature Horatianized. Nevertheless, Pope and his friends—writers, statesmen, artists, country gentlemen of many degrees of grandeur—often saw their own world through Horace's eyes and to a surprising degree tried to shape the actuality to fit the dream. The eighteenth-century villa, not too far from Town, stocked with the best authors and provided with a beautiful and useful garden, is "translated" out of Horace. Pope's house at "Twitnam" is the charming if amusing symbol of a life and a literary career that became progressively an *Imitatio Horati*.[5]

R. M. Ogilvie devotes some three and a half pages to further parallels between the two ages and cultures, clearly readier than Professor Brower, whom he quotes in part, to see more and more deeply-rooted similarities in the political, social, economic, and literary atmosphere and activities of the two eras.[6] But whether the similarities were really there or whether they were largely superficial and retrospectively made to seem greater because Pope and Prior and, as Mr. Ogilvie suggests, the famous men of the third quarter of the eighteenth century consciously cast themselves as neo-Augustans, there is no denying that Horace and the world and life he wrote about were dear to eighteenth-century Englishmen. Professor Brower goes so far as to suggest that "for the small yet influential class that created what we call eighteenth-century civilization, Horace was a kind of 'cultural hero'" (p. 163).

However much literary, and literate, men of the eighteenth century may have enjoyed picturing themselves as latter-day Horaces, the extent of the Roman poet's influence in England in this period is seen most dramatically in translations and imitations of his poetry. Indeed, the latter, as exemplified by Pope's "Imitations from Horace," became virtually a separate genre. Samuel Johnson, animadverting upon Pope's efforts, presented an excellent definition and critical appraisal of it:

> This mode of imitation, in which the ancients are familiarised, by adapting their sentiments to modern topics, by making Horace say of Shakespeare what he originally said of Ennius, and accommodating his satires on Pantolabus and Nomentanus to the flatterers and prodigals of our own time, was first practised in the reign of Charles the Second by Oldham and Rochester; at least I remember no instances more ancient. It is a kind of middle composition between translation and original design, which pleases when the thoughts are unexpectedly applicable, and the parallels lucky. It seems to have been Pope's favourite amusement, for he has carried it farther than any former poet. . . .

> The *Imitations of Horace* seem to have been written as relaxations of his genius. This employment became his favourite by its facility; the plan was ready to his hand, and nothing was required but to accommodate as he could the sentiments of an old author to recent facts or familiar images; but what is easy is seldom excellent; such imitations cannot give pleasure to common readers. The man of learning may be sometimes surprised and delighted by an unexpected parallel; but the comparison requires knowledge of the original, which will likewise often detect strained applications. Between Roman images and English manners there will be an irreconcileable dissimilitude, and the works will be generally uncouth and party-coloured; neither original nor translated, neither ancient nor modern.[7]

Pope's formal "imitations" are unmistakably identified, both by their titles, *The First Satire of the Second Book of Horace* or *Epistles of Horace Book I, Epistle I*, and by the appearance of the Latin of the original *en face*. Johnson, an "imitator" of Juvenal, furnished most of the text of the third Satire of that Latin poet with his *London* and gave line references to Juvenal's tenth Satire at the bottom of the page with his *Vanity of Human Wishes*. He insisted that those paragraphs of Juvenal that he had most closely followed in *London* "must be subjoined at the bottom of the page, part of the beauty of the performance (if any beauty be allowed it) consisting in adapting Juvenal's sentiments to modern facts and persons." Obviously, however familiar one's readers could be presumed to be with the Latin of the poem being "imitated," it was thought well to have the full text of the original, or at least enough of it to recall subsequent lines of the context of a particular passage. Whatever Johnson's opinion of the genre as a whole, and he wrote the life of Pope some thirty years after *The Vanity of Human Wishes* (his second "imitation" of Juvenal), he has made further definition unnecessary. And possibly he used the heaviest weapon in his critical artillery when he flatly stated that "such imitations cannot give pleasure to common readers."

John Dryden, writing a century before Johnson, in a famous passage in the Preface to the translation of Ovid's *Epistles*, distinguishes three kinds of translation, of which

> the third way is that of imitation, where the translator (if now he has not lost that name) assumes the liberty, not only to vary from the words and sense, but to forsake them both as he sees occasion, and taking only some general hints from the original, to run division on the groundwork, as he pleases. Such is Mr. Cowley's practice in turning two Odes of Pindar, and one of Horace, into English.

He returns to the subject again, and speaking of Abraham Cowley and Sir John Denham, redefines or re-explains "imitation":

> I take imitation of an author, in their sense, to be an endeavour of a later poet to write like one who has written before him, on the same subject; that is, not to translate his words, or to be confined to his sense, but only to set him as a pattern, and to write, as he supposed that author would have done, had he lived in our age, and in our country.[8]

Cowley translated, as had Milton before him, the very popular fifth *Ode* of Horace's first Book, *Ad Pyrrham*. Where a literal prose translation of the first four and a half lines of the Latin is rendered as "What slender youth, bedewed with perfumes, embraces thee amid many a rose, O Pyrrha, in the pleasant grotto? For whom dost thou tie up thy golden hair in simple elegance?" Cowley has

> To whom now, *Pyrrha*, art thou kinde?
> To what heart-ravisht Lover
> Dost thou thy golden locks unbinde,
> Thy hidden sweets discover,
> And with large bounty open set
> All the bright stores of thy rich *Cabinet*?[9]

More striking as an example of "imitation" is the collaboration between Cowley and Thomas Sprat on a version of Horace's famous sixth Satire of the second Book for which Cowley provided only the concluding fable of the city mouse and the country mouse. Sprat generously and judiciously rang in allusions to English matters and figures in his part of the poem.[10]

9

Pope, of whom Professor Brower writes that "nearly everything" he wrote after his translation of the *Iliad* "shows more or less distinctly the influence of Horatian poetic modes and themes" (p. 165), was the most successful practitioner of the formal "imitation." However, he also wrote poems which, while they capture much of the spirit and tone of Horace, do not take a specific poem and "imitate" it. The *Epistle to Dr. Arbuthnot* and the *Epilogue to the Satires* are neither imitations in this last sense nor in the Cowleian sense as defined by Dryden and exemplified by the former's "translation" of *Ad Pyrrham.* Rather, they represent a third and more widespread kind of influence exerted by Horace's poetry, deriving from the tone, techniques, and themes in his poetry. Thus they form a body of eighteenth-century verse that owes nearly everything to Horace's poetry as a whole and almost nothing to any single poem.

One has, then, three modes showing Horatian influence. First there is the formal "imitation," in which Rome becomes London, and Augustus becomes whatever monarch is reigning in England at the time. Then there is Cowley's brand of imitation or translation, which has affinities with the formal "imitation" but departs more freely from its original. Poems in the third mode do not treat specific subjects dealt with by Horace but nonetheless call him to mind—this is what is meant when a poet is described as having the Horatian manner.

Matthew Prior, possibly more than any other English poet except Pope, managed the Horatian manner with the least constraint and the most endearing results. However, his happiest efforts were not those in which he chose to "imitate" a particular poem by Horace. Of four such "imitations," only one, *Horace Lib. I Epist. IX . . . Imitated*, has any real merit. Where Horace had introduced Septimius to Nero, Prior recommends a friend in need of a place to Robert Harley.

> Dear Dick, how e'er it comes into his Head,
> Believes, as firmly as He does his Creed,
> That You and I, SIR, are extremely great;
> Tho' I plain MAT, You *Minister of State.*
> One Word from Me, without all doubt, He says,
> Wou'd fix his Fortune in some little Place.
> Thus better than My self, it seems, He knows,
> How far my Interest with my Patron goes;
> And answering all Objections I can make,
> Still plunges deeper in his dear Mistake.
>
> From this wild Fancy, SIR, there may proceed
> One wilder yet, which I foresee, and dread;
> That I, in Fact, a real Interest have,
> Which to my own Advantage I wou'd save,

> And, with the usual Courtier's Trick, intend
> To serve My self, forgetful of my Friend.
>
>> To shun this Censure, I all Shame lay by;
>> And make my Reason with his Will Comply;
>> Hoping, for my Excuse, 'twill be confest,
>> That of two Evils I have chose the least.
>> So, SIR, with this Epistolary Scroll,
>> Receive the Partner of my inmost Soul:
>> Him you will find in Letters, and in Laws
>> Not unexpert, firm to his Country's Cause,
>> Warm in the Glorious Interest You pursue,
>> And, in one Word, a Good Man and a True.

When Christopher Smart later translated the twenty-eighth Ode of the first Book for his 1767 verse translation, he appended a footnote, "See this ode finely imitated by Matthew Prior." This reinforces my belief that he much admired and was influenced by Prior's poetry, but it does little for Smart's reputation as a critic. For one thing, Prior's poem is only very loosely an "imitation," and for another it is not poetry of a high order. And it should be added that in another of the four poems, his *Carmen Seculare*, his "imitation" extends only to the title and the general theme.

But it was in his short lyrics that Prior caught Horace's air and tone. These are the poems for which he is best remembered, poems in a largely facetious vein with some admixture of seriousness, addressed to one woman or another whom he loves, has loved, or is being unfaithful to—although, of course, he protests that he really loves only her. Like Horace before him, Prior addresses many of his poems to a number of pseudonymous women. Horace has his Lydia; Prior has his Cloe; Horace has his Pyrrha, Lalage, and Glycera; Prior has his Lisetta, Phyllis, and Celia. Both have trouble with their women, both try to reason patiently with them. Prior, it will be recalled, faced with the need to placate the jealous Cloe, wrote one "Answer" to her and then still another and "Better Answer." The latter ends,

>> Then finish, Dear CLOE, this Pastoral War;
>> And let us like HORACE and LYDIA agree:
>> For Thou art a Girl as much brighter than Her,
>> As He was a Poet sublimer than Me.

A further indication of Horace's appeal to Prior's fancy lies in the opening lines of the poem, *Written in the Year 1696*,

>> While with Labour Assiduous due pleasure I mix
>> And in one day attone for the Busyness of Six

11

> In a little Dutch Chaise on a Saturday Night
> On my left hand my Horace, a Nymph on my right.

Pope was also "a poet sublimer" than Prior, but I doubt that he was more addicted to Horace. In the matter of "nymphs" there can be no controversy; this was Prior's metier.

A partial index to the popularity of Horace's poems can be had from an examination of the poetry section of the *Gentleman's Magazine* for the first fifty-six years (1731-1786) of its existence. Imitations, translations, "paraphrases," and poems "taken from Horace" range over the four Books of *Odes*; they also include four *Epistles*, seven *Epodes*, and one *Satire*. Within the admittedly narrow confines of criteria drawn only from one periodical, there is additional evidence of the popularity of particular poems. The following table is based on the index to the poetry in the *Gentleman's Magazine* for the period indicated; the number in parentheses gives the total occurrences of the poem in question. There are thirty-eight *Odes* in the first Book, twenty in the second, thirty in the third, and fifteen in the fourth.

> *Odes*, Bk. I. i (5), ii (3), iii (3), iv, v (3), vi (2), vii (2), ix (2), xi, xiii, xiv (2), xv, xvii, xviii, xix, xxii (4), xxiii (2), xxiv (2), xxv, xxix, xxxi, xxxii, xxxiii (2), xxxiv (2), xxxvii
> *Odes*, Bk. II. i, ii (3), iii (4), iv (5), vi, vii, x (4), xi, xiv (4), xvi (8), xvii, xxviii
> *Odes*, Bk. III. i, ii, iii, vi, viii, ix (4), x, xiii (2), xix (2), xxi
> *Odes*, Bk. IV. ii, iii (2), v, vii, viii, x, xiii
> *Epistles*, Bk. I. v (2), vi, x
> *Satires*, Bk. II. iii
> *Epodes*, ii (5), xiii, xv

To this should be added another dozen entries for "odes of Horace translated and imitated" that appear without further identification. While the absence in the index of any translations or imitations of the *Carmen Seculare* is not astonishing, the absence as well of anything from or based on the *Art of Poetry* is strange, given the popularity it is said to have enjoyed. Possibly its length gave pause, and imitators were loath to try their art on select passages only. If the number of times a single poem was imitated or translated is a reliable criterion, the favorites in this period were *Odes* II. xvi, *Otium divos rogat* (8); I. 1. *Mæcenas atavis edite regibus* (5); II. iv. *Ne sit ancillae* (5); *Epodes*, ii, *Beatus ille*, on country joys (5); and with four occurrences each, *Odes*, I. xxii, *Integer vitæ*; II. ii, *Nullus argento color*; II. x, *Rectius vives*; II. xiv, *Eheu fugaces*; and III. ix, *Donec gratus*.

Once the very popular tenth *Ode* of the second Book—advocating the "golden mean"—is "paraphrased" and "address'd to a young gentleman of Liverpool"; at another time the fourteenth *Ode* of the first Book is "paraphrased and inscribed to the Church of England" and Horace's ship of state becomes "O Church of England's ship." Still further evidence that the *Gentleman's* readers and contributors had Horace much in mind is the following from 1744:

> The late foggy weather should have put some of your bright correspondents in mind of a compliment of Horace to Augustus, and applicable to the Cæsar of Great Britain with remarkable propriety. I wish Philargyrus would oblige us with a translation of the whole.

The writer thereupon quotes the second four lines of the fifth *Ode* of the fourth Book and offers his translation—actually his imitation—of them. On a few occasions English poems are written "in imitation of" Horatian originals which are identified solely by quotation of a line. Evidently there was no need further to identify their source. As slight additional evidence of the interest in Horace in this period the *Gentleman's* index of essays contains twenty-two entries for Horace. For the same period there are but eight entries for Juvenal and there are only two imitations and one translation of parts of his satires in the poetry columns for the fifty-six years.

R. M. Ogilvie's statement that "although Horace was also read as a lyric poet and still provided inspiration for poets like Gray and Collins it was as a satirist that he made his appeal" (p. 50) is greatly at variance with the pitifully poor showing the *Satires* and *Epistles* make in the foregoing analysis. And the *Gentleman's Magazine*, it must be borne in mind, was the most popular periodical of the century. Miss Goad is also inclined to give what is, to my mind, undue weight to the influence of Horace's *Satires* and *Epistles* on eighteenth-century periodical essayists. She speaks of the series of periodical essays from the *Tatler* and *Spectator* through Johnson's *Rambler* as "an eighteenth-century rejuvenation of Horace's Satires and Epistles" and points out that "the fact that Horace was the favorite author for the mottoes with which almost all these papers began their lucubrations, rather than Juvenal on the one hand, or Virgil on the other, is evidence that their writers were conscious of his special value and significance to them" (p. 8). She might here have quoted Arthur Murphy in one of his *Gray's-Inn Journal* essays:

> My readers will observe, that the mottos to these essays are frequently selected from the author, whose name stands at the head of this day's paper. Horace is the writer of all antiquity, who looked at life with an eye of penetration; and has painted the manners and the passions of men with the most elegant touches

of his art. His sense is so refined, and the turn of his expression so peculiarly delicate, that his remarks occur upon almost every occasion. He is sensibly and elegantly sententious, not only in his epistles and satires, which are professedly moral discourses, but also in his lighter odes, and his gayest excursions of fancy. I have often thought that an excellent system of morality might be extracted out of his writings; and I have carried this hint so far, as to think seriously of publishing a translation of all his excellent ethic observations, which would, in my opinion, be the best collection of thoughts on various subjects, that has ever been offered to the public.[11]

Inspection of the mottoes to the *Spectator* reveals 76 uses of the *Epistles*, 54 of the *Art of Poetry*, 51 of the *Odes*, and 39 of the *Satires*; the first *Epode* provides a motto for essay number 328. Juvenal, with a much smaller corpus of work than Horace, does quite well as the source of 48 mottoes. Thus, while Miss Goad is right in the main, one must discount neither the possible influence of Juvenal nor of Horace's *Odes* on the writers of the *Spectator*. Later in the century, and, in the hands of a writer who had chosen to "imitate" Juvenal rather than Horace in his own poetry, only eight *Rambler* mottoes come from Horace.[12] For whatever it may be worth, it is well to recall that, either through academic necessity or for his own amusement, Samuel Johnson as a youth translated two of Horace's *Epodes* and three of the *Odes*. And a month before his death he turned to Horace again and translated the seventh *Ode* of the fourth Book, *Diffugere nives.*

Johnson told Boswell that "Horace's *Odes* were the compositions in which he took most delight, and it was long before he liked his *Epistles* and *Satires.*" I am not sure, knowing as much about Johnson's life and character as we do, that such a preference could have been conjectured. When one reads Johnson's considered opinion that "the peculiarity of Juvenal is a mixture of gaiety and stateliness, of pointed sentences, and declamatory grandeur," it is fairly easy to understand why he took him as a model when he wrote his two verse satires.[13] Less easy to understand is Johnson's fondness, early and late, for Horace's *Odes*. Except for the sombre *Diffugere nives*, translated shortly before his death, the remaining *Odes* and *Epodes* he translated dealt with such traditionally poetic subjects as the joys of rural life (*Epode* II), the power of love (*Epode* XI), the immortality of the poet (*Odes*, II. xx), the folly of continued sorrow (*Odes*, II. ix), and the passage of time (*Eheu fugaces*, *Odes*, II. xiv). Since these last five translations are juvenilia, some allowance must be made for Johnson's probable desire to work in traditional themes. Unless, of course, they were school exercises and he had no choice but to translate these particular poems. The point is that Horace is almost invariably described as urbane; he evidently was, or gives the impression of being, a ladies' man; he loved his country retreat and he maintained a long although admittedly not servile relationship with a rich patron of the arts. Now none of this, one would think, would particularly endear him to Johnson, and it is not, hence, surprising that the fine raillery, the informality of manner and language, and the preoccupation with the follies of men rather than with their vices that characterized Horace's satiric poems should also cause Johnson to look elsewhere for a more appropriate model for "imitation." Horace's poetry had the power to charm Johnson; the *Life* abounds with quotations from virtually the whole corpus of Horace's poetry. But it was Juvenal whom he imitated.

When Johnson's *London* was published anonymously in May 1738 it had to compete with an imitation of Horace written by England's leading poet. Alexander Pope's *One Thousand Seven Hundred and Thirty Eight. Dialogue II* appeared three days after *London* was published, "so that," as Boswell puts it, "England had at once its Juvenal and Horace as poetical monitors" (*Life*, I, 127). Almost exactly nine years before this, Elijah Fenton, in a letter to William Broome, wrote that Pope "told me that for the future he intended to write nothing but epistles in Horace's manner, in which I question not but he will succeed very well."[14] Pope succeeded so well that among other testimonies to his skill in imitating Horace may be added his own. His imitation of Horace's second *Satire* of the first Book was published in December 1734 with the title *Sober Advice From Horace* and the words "Imitated in the Manner of Mr. Pope," a bit of self-advertising that prevented him from acknowledging the poem as his own, although he later thought nothing of giving it a place in his octavo *Works.* While Pope's "imitations" of Horace are justly acclaimed as supreme of their kind, it was not, I believe, because he was temperamentally a great deal like Horace. He had his villa and he lived in a rather easy intimacy with the rich and noble, but there the similarities end.[15] Like Horace, however, he was a highly skillful craftsman as well as a great poet, and he could adopt Horatian themes and techniques with an ease and mastery that were given to very few other English poets. If one can imagine the genius of Pope joined with the temperament of Prior, one would then have an English Horace who might contend with his Roman prototype for poetic honors.

Preoccupation with Horace's poetry was not, of course, limited to poets; indeed, the poets, to a certain extent, depended on the translators. Not that the poets could not translate Horace for themselves, but it was so much easier to turn to an available translation and take it as a point of departure for one's own version of a word, a line, or a passage. So, too, with the writers of periodical essays. The name most frequently encountered in the translations of lines from Horace used as mottoes to the *Spectator* essays is that of Thomas Creech. Creech was best known for his very popular translation of Lucretius, although, before he took his own life in 1700, he had translated, among other works, parts of Ovid, Plutarch, Theocritus, Juvenal, and Cornelius Nepos. And, of course, he had translated Horace's *Odes, Satires,* and *Epistles,* in 1684. While opinion about his skills as a translator of Horace varied,[16] his version of the *Odes, Satires,* and *Epistles* held its own against rivals until the mid-eighteenth century, editions of his translation appearing in 1688, 1711, 1715, 1718, 1720, 1730, 1737, and so on. Of a collaborative translation of Juvenal's satires directed by Dryden, in which Creech's part was the thirteenth Satire, Samuel Johnson wrote, "His grandeur none of the band seemed to consider as necessary to be imitated, except Creech" (*Lives,* I, 447). Added to this evidence of Johnson's estimate of Creech's abilities is the fact that later Johnson used Creech's translation for a number of the mottoes and quotations from Horace in his *Rambler* essays, even though other versions were available to him and even though he translated a number of them himself. Creech's translation of Horace was the only complete one available to Pope, who did not hesitate to borrow a few felicitous renderings of words or even, in one instance, a whole line from him.[17] Creech was aware of the difficulties that confronted the translator, whether of Horace or any other poet, and he quite frankly outlined in his Preface what he hoped he had accomplished in translating Horace and what he had not even attempted. "'Tis certain," he writes, "our Language is not Capable of the numbers of the Poet, and therefore if the sense of the Author is deliver'd, the variety of the Expression kept, . . . and his Fancy not debas'd, . . . 'tis all that can be expected from a version."

Others, early and late, shared Creech's conviction that it was useless to try to recreate Horace's "numbers" in English verse, but they, unlike him, took the more drastic step of rendering his poems into English prose. Smart's first attempt at translating Horace's works was in the latter category, but he could point to the earlier prose versions of Samuel Dunster in 1709, Leonard Welsted in 1726 (in six volumes), David Watson in 1741, Matthew Towers in 1742-43, Patrick Samuel in 1743, and John Stirling in 1751-53. Some of these prose versions, like Smart's, were, one hopes, intended as school texts; an edition of 1751 bears the title, "The Works of Horace. With the Original Text. And reduc'd to the Natural Order of Construction with Accents to regulate the right Pronunciation, and a close and truly literal English Translation, rendering that Author exceedingly easy and familiar to every Reader. In a Method never attempted before, for the Use of all Lovers of the Prince of Lyrics." Almost the sole endeavor of these translators of Horace into prose was to be as faithful as possible to their original; literal translation into verse had been discredited for some time—at least as early as 1636, when Sir John Denham's translation of the second book of the *Æneid* was published. Johnson in his life of Denham praised him for "emancipating translation from the drudgery of counting lines and interpreting single words" (*Lives*, I, 79).

Still other poets and translators, recognizing the critical hot water they could get into by attempting to translate all or a large part of Horace's work single-handedly, clubbed together in an edition. On occasion, efforts were made by some enterprising spirit to produce translations "by the most eminent hands," or a variation upon that formula. The very popular and often reprinted 1715 edition has a long informative title that reads, "The Odes and Satires of Horace, That have been done by the most Eminent Hands, viz. Lord Rochester, Lord Roscommon, Mr. Cowley, Mr. Otway, Mr. Congreve, Mr. Prior, Mr. Maynwaring, And several others. With his Art of Poetry, By My Lord Roscommon." Should the prospective buyer not already be dazzled by the constellation of literary greats represented on the title page, a look at the table of contents would also reveal the inclusion as translators of such other notables as Sir Richard Steele and Sir William Temple. The name of my Lord Roscommon would carry some added reassurance and weight as to the worth of the translations, for he had written a verse *Essay on Translated Verse* and could hence be regarded as something of an authority both as to precept and practice. Among other injunctions in his *Essay on Translated Verse* is the following:

> Examine how your Humour is inclined,
> And which the Ruling Passion of your Mind;
> Then, seek a Poet who your way do's bend,
> And chuse an Author as you chuse a Friend.

Dryden, whose analysis of translation remained a standard for most of the eighteenth century, said much the same in his "Preface to the Translation of Ovid's Epistles" (1680):

> No man is capable of translating poetry, who, besides a genius to that art, is not a master both of his author's language, and of his own; nor must we understand the language only of the poet, but his particular turn of thoughts and expression, which are the characters that distinguish, and as it were individuate him from all other writers. When we are come this far, 'tis time to look into ourselves, to conform our genius to his, to give his thought either the same turn, if our tongue will bear it, or, if not, to vary but the dress, not to alter or destroy the substance.[18]

How much Horace's various English translators could be said to fulfil these rather stringent conditions remains questionable. Five years after the translation of Ovid's *Epistles*, Dryden examined the whole matter of translation even more thoroughly. His Preface to *Sylvæ* (1685) begins, rather delightfully, with the statement, "For this last half year I have been troubled with the disease (as I may call it) of translation; the cold prose fits of it, which are always the most tedious with me, were spent in the *History of the League*: the hot, which succeeded them, in this volume of Verse Miscellanies." He pays his ironic *devoirs* to Roscommon's *Essay on Translated Verse* and then he goes off on his own. Returning to the precept he had laid down five years earlier, he states that

> it appears necessary, that a man should be a nice critic in his mother-tongue before he attempts to translate a foreign language. Neither is it sufficient that he be able to judge of words and style; but he must be a master of them too; he must perfectly understand his author's tongue, and absolutely command his own. So that to be a thorough translator, he must be a thorough poet. Nor is it enough to give his author's sense in good English, in poetical expressions, and in musical numbers; for though all these are exceeding difficult to perform, there yet remains a harder task; and 'tis a secret of which few translators have sufficiently thought. I have already hinted a word or two concerning it; that is, the maintaining the character of an author, which distinguished him from all others, and makes him appear that individual poet whom you would interpret.[19]

And since he had translated a few of Horace's odes in *Sylvae* he took it upon himself to characterize that poet's style and tone. Of the first he mentioned the "elegance of his words," the "numerousness"[20] of his verse, the "noble and bold purity" of his diction, and, of course, the "secret happiness" which attends his choice of words, i.e., his *curiosa felicitas.* As for what I have chosen to call the tone of Horace's poetry Dryden says, "But the most distinguishing part of his character seems to me to be his briskness, his jollity, and his good humour."[21] He is speaking, it is well to remember, solely of Horace's odes.

From the facts of Creech's life it would be difficult to think of a person less likely to be a kindred spirit to Horace. Yet despite Roscommon's and Dryden's belief in this necessary compatibility between translator and the poet he elects to translate, Creech's version of the *Odes, Satires,* and *Epistles,* as I have already indicated, enjoyed lasting popularity. Not until the appearance of Philip Francis's translation of the *Odes, Epodes,* and *Carmen Seculare* in 1743, with the addition of the *Satires, Epistles,* and *Art of Poetry* in 1746, was Creech's version supplanted. Boswell records Johnson's opinion that "the lyrical part of Horace never can be perfectly translated; so much of the excellence is in the numbers and expression. Francis has done it the best; I'll take his, five out of six, against them all" (*Life*, III, 356). As did most of his predecessors, Francis wrote a Preface to his translation. In it, after stating that "if we may rely upon the Judgement of his Commentators, he has united in his Lyric Poetry the Enthusiasm of Pindar, the Majesty of Alcæus, the Tenderness of Sappho, and the charming Levities of Anacreon," Francis could be pardoned his plea that "surely the best Attempts to translate so various an Author, will require great indulgence, and any tolerable Success may deserve it." He did not minimize the other difficulties that confronted the translator of Horace, especially that of rendering both the letter and the spirit of his original. And he devoted some time to explaining his attempts to find appropriate stanzaic and metric forms for what he termed "the numerous Variety of Measures" in Horace's *Odes*. All in all, his was a very creditable translation by eighteenth-century standards, and when William Duncombe and his son John published the first of a two-volume translation of Horace in 1757, the reviewer for the *Monthly Review*, in the issue for January 1758, devoted as much time to praising Francis's version as he did to examining the Duncombes'. "That gentleman's version," he wrote of Francis, "particularly of the *Odes*, is highly Horatian: it is moral without whining. Hence few translations have gone through more editions, or met with greater applause from the public" (p. 45). Whoever undertook to translate Horace would have Francis's very popular version to contend with.

A conscientious translator was faced with the decision to choose from among a number of available edited texts of Horace's poetry. Most famous of those to which Philip Francis and Smart had access was Richard Bentley's. The irascible Master of Trinity College, Cambridge, began thinking around 1702 about an edition of some author "of the pleasanter sort, comparatively light in style and matter . . . a work that could be done bit by bit at odd hours. . . . My choice was Horace."[22] Bentley's *Horace* was published on December 8, 1711, to coincide with the birthday of the Latin poet; more than any other work of the century, it focused attention on Horace's text. For Bentley made between seven and eight hundred emendations in a text that has always been considered "particularly pure," to use Jebb's words. Despite Bentley's enormous erudition and because of his arrogance, his fulsome praise of his own efforts, and the contempt with which he treated the work of other scholars, the edition of Horace was immediately and frequently attacked, usually anonymously.

The most notable of these attacks was *The Odes of Horace in Latin and English: With a Translation of Dr. Bentley's Notes. To which are added Notes upon Notes; Done in the Bentleian Style and Manner*, published in parts at sixpence the part. Seventeen parts were published in 1712; three more in 1713 completed the work. But, also in 1713, four more parts were added, given over to a translation of the *Epodes* and the *Carmen Seculare*. Although advertised as "by several hands," a second edition in 1719 identified William Oldisworth as the translator.[23] Bentley, impervious to these attacks, had a second edition of his *Horace* published in Amsterdam in 1713; a third was published in that same city in 1728. Only one attempt was made to rival his edition: Alexander Cunningham, a Scottish scholar of some renown, published an edition in 1721.[24] But it was Bentley's *Horace* that continued to be the standard text for many years to come; there were added editions or reprints in 1740, 1743, and 1764. And it was the impetus given by his work that was responsible for the renewed scholarly attention directed toward Horace's poetry. Once, at least, Christopher Smart came face to face with the aging Master of Trinity College, for on June 1, 1742, only a month and a half before Bentley's death, Smart was examined and elected to one of two University Scholarships established by Lord Craven. Bentley was one of the examiners and electors on that occasion.[25]

II.

The precise time at which Christopher Smart (1722-71) was made aware of a body of Latin poetry by a certain Quintus Horatius Flaccus it is impossible to ascertain. His formal education began in the free grammar school in Maidstone, Kent, under Charles Walwyn of Eton and King's College, Cambridge, at the latter of which Walwyn proceeded to an M.A. in 1696. With Walwyn, Smart would have learned the rudiments of Latin grammar and would have begun translating Latin prose into English. But it was almost surely not until he went to Durham Grammar School at the age of eleven that he began to read and translate Horace's poetry. At Durham the headmaster was Richard Dongworth, another Etonian, who had been a Fellow of Magdalene College, Cambridge, before he removed to the north. Contemporary references to Dongworth stress his learning and scholarship, and it is logical to assume that his influence on Smart in the six years, 1733 to 1739, that the latter attended Durham Grammar School was deep and lasting. Of this period Christopher Hunter, Smart's nephew and biographer, wrote, "Smart did not continue without distinction at Durham School; and a very learned and eminent Divine, now living, has expressed obligations to our Author for his own first successful essays in Latin versification."[26] Evidently, by the time Smart left Durham for Cambridge, he not only had achieved considerable facility in writing Latin verse but had also helped others in their attempts. Smart later had the habit of resurrecting his early poetry to fill up an issue of one of the many literary enterprises that kept him feverishly busy in his London years; some of these, in Latin, were written while he was still at Durham.[27] Again, it is impossible to know whether he was imitating or translating Horace for his own purposes at this time; that he was reading and translating Horace as part of the curriculum at Durham Grammar School may be taken for granted. Horace occupied a prominent place in the curriculum of English grammar schools, and Durham was no exception.

When Smart entered Pembroke College, Cambridge, in 1739 he had probably learned as much Latin as he ever would, for while his reading in Latin authors probably widened, his knowledge of the language itself advanced but little. One was assumed to have a fairly good knowledge of Latin by the time he entered a university. Hunter tells us that his uncle's "classical attainments and poetical powers were so eminent, as to attract the notice of persons, not very strongly prejudiced in favor of such accomplishments" (p.viii). He was chosen to write the Latin Tripos verses three years in a row, and he also won the prestigious and lucrative Craven Scholarship in 1742. For both honors he had to demonstrate, or have demonstrated, his ability to handle Latin with ease. Another example of that same ease is seen in a Latin poem he wrote to Samuel Saunders, a friend at King's College, in a metre used with some frequency by Horace.[28]

In 1743 Smart was asked to write a poem to commemorate the foundation of Pembroke College four hundred years earlier, and he obliged with his "Secular Ode on the Jubilee at Pembroke-College, Cambridge," which borrows its title from Horace's *Carmen Seculare* and begins, as does Horace's poem, by invoking a number of deities; there the similarities cease. Also in 1743, this time in spontaneous and lighthearted celebration of receiving his Bachelor's degree, he turned to the thirtieth *Ode* of Horace's third Book, *Exegi monumentum ære perennius*, as a point of departure for a poem on the joys of freedom. When, seven years later, the poem was printed in *The Student*, which Smart was helping to edit, it carried a number of the lines of Horace's ode in the margin. No chance was taken that Smart's clever twisting of Horace's lines might be missed. Closest of all to Horace in this period was Smart's "imitation" of the thirteenth *Ode* of the fourth Book (twelfth in his numbering), *Audivere, Lyce, Dii mea vota*, in which the Roman jeers at the faded beauty Lyce. Here is what Smart makes of it:

> At length Mother Gunter the Gods hear my prayer,
> They have heard me at length, Mother Gunter,
> You're grown an old Woman yet romp drink and swear,
> And attest the tricks of Pounter.
>
> You invoke with a voice that tremblingly squeaks
> Brisk Cupid tho sure of denial;
> He Shuns you and basks in the blossomly cheeks
> Of Miss Gubbins who plays on the Viol.

He flies from the trunk that is sapless and bare
To the pliant young Branches he comes up;
Age has hail'd on thy face, and has snow'd on thy hair,
And thy green Teeth have eat all thy Gums up.

Nor thy Sack, nor thy Necklace, thy watch, nor thy Ring,
Have restored thee to youth, or retarded
Those years which Old Time and his friend Vincent Wing
In the Almanack long have recorded.

O where is that beauty, that bloom and that grace,
Those lips that would breath Inspiration,
That steal me away from myself, and gave place,
To no Creature save Joan in the nation.

But poor Joan is dead, and has left you her years
As a Legacy which gracious Heaven
Has join'd to your own, which a Century clears,
And is just Mad'm the age of a Raven.

There remains a memento to each jolly soul,
Who of Venus's Club's a staunch member,
That Love hot as fire must be burnt to a coal,
As the Broomstick concludes in an Ember.

Some time late in 1749 Smart, deep in debt and in disgrace because of persistent drunkenness, moved to London hoping to make his way by his pen; he had had enough of academic existence after ten years as student and Fellow at Pembroke College. He had already had poems published in some of the London periodicals, and he had begun a correspondence with the bookseller Robert Dodsley. In a letter dated January 30, 1746/7, he told Dodsley that he had "imitated a satyr of Horace in the manner of Pope," further evidence both of his interest in Horace and of the influence of Pope's "imitations." Smart's imitation, *The Horatian Canons of Friendship*, which had to wait until 1750 to be published, is of the third *Satire* of the first Book. While there is no gainsaying that Pope did this sort of thing much better, Smart's effort manages a lively, colloquial tone that does justice to its source. Where Horace, as translated in the Loeb version, has, "If a boy squints, his father calls him 'Blinky,'" Smart takes four lines:

The Sire, whose Son squints forty thousand Ways,
Finds in his Features mighty Room for Praise:
'Ah! born' (he cries) 'to make the Ladies sigh,
Jacky, thou hast an am'rous cast o' th'Eye.'

With Horace's Latin poem printed with it, the reader was again invited to admire the cleverness employed in bringing Roman times and personages up to date. A few months after the publication of the *Horatian Canons*, Smart had begun writing most of the contents of a periodical called *The Midwife*. In the July 1751 issue of this magazine, having already written a number of pieces under the pseudonym Ebenezer Pentweazle, he became for one occasion Nelly Pentweazle, niece to Mrs. Mary Midnight, his known pseudonym as editor of *The Midwife*. The occasion was a translation into English of Horace's first *Ode* of the first Book, *Mæcenas atavis edite regibus*, whose thirty-six lines are spun to twice their length in the *Song to David* stanza that Smart was to make famous.

Smart's real bid for poetic fame appeared in 1752 in the form of an elegantly printed *Poems on Several Occasions*, which he had been preparing for at least the nine years Horace had given as the desirable time to age a piece of literature. In fact, Horace's words to this effect are quoted on the title page. The volume contains one more poem in the series which found inspiration in Horace's. This time Smart went to the fourth *Ode* of the second Book, *Ne sit ancillae tibi amor pudori*, entitling his poem *The Pretty Chambermaid*. The "imitation," so labelled by Smart, is a fine one; the reader may wish to compare it with the version in Smart's verse *Horace*:

Colin, oh! cease thy friend to blame,
Who entertains a servile flame.
Chide not—believe me, 'tis no more
Than great Achilles did before,
Who nobler, prouder far than he is,
Ador'd his chambermaid Briseis.

The thund'ring Ajax Venus lays
In love's inextricable maze.
His slave Tecmessa makes him yield,
Now mistress of the sevenfold shield.
Atrides with his captive play'd,
Who always shar'd the bed she made.

'Twas at the ten years siege, when all
The Trojans fell in Hector's fall,
When Helen rul'd the day and night,
And made them love and made them fight;
Each hero kiss'd his maid, and why,
Tho' I'm no hero, may not I?

Who knows? Polly perhaps may be
A piece of ruin'd royalty.
She has (I cannot doubt it) been

23

The daughter of some mighty queen;
But fate's irremeable doom
Has chang'd her sceptre for a broom.

Ah! cease to think it—how can she,
So generous, charming, fond, and free,
So lib'ral of her little store,
So heedless of amassing more,
Have one drop of plebeian blood
In all the circulating flood?

But you, by carping at my fire,
Do but betray your own desire—
Howe'er proceed—made tame by years,
You'll raise in me no jealous fears.
You've not one spark of love alive,
For, thanks to heav'n, you're forty-five.

Although Horace's Latin did not appear in the 1752 volume, Hunter saw fit to include it in his 1791 edition of Smart's poems. Up to this time, then, Smart had "imitated" three *Odes* and a *Satire* of Horace, "translated" one *Ode*, and written a "secular ode" very remotely deriving from the *Carmen Seculare*.

That Smart turned to Horace for a poetic model may be put down to three causes, all of considerable though not equal importance in his development as a poet and translator. First, and least important, was the fact that Pope—whose poetic accomplishments Smart virtually reverenced—had written a number of "imitations" of Horace, and I have a growing suspicion that Smart was patterning himself on Pope, trying the genres Pope had written in—at least up to a certain point in his own career. In addition, there is the great popularity and widespread influence of Horace during this period. Finally, and I am not sure whether this takes precedence over Horace's popularity, there is the fact that certain similarities exist between the lives of Horace and Smart. Obviously I do not wish to push these resemblances too far, but I would offer the following for consideration. Both men were of modest origin; Horace's father was a freedman who attained a position which enabled him to have his son educated at Rome and Athens. Smart, despite his contention that his family was of the nobility, was the son of the steward on the Kentish estate of the Vane family; he was educated at Durham and Cambridge. Although they had seen and lived in other parts of their respective countries, in their poetry both men turned most often and with pride to the sights and sounds and traditions of their native place, Venusia for Horace and that part of Kent near Maidstone for Smart. At school they were thrown in with young men who were of wealthier and nobler origin; references to this appear in their poetry. At some time both had known what it was to be poor and forced to write for money; *paupertas impulit audax ut versus facerem* ("impelled by want I become a poet") wrote Horace retrospectively in the last of his *Epistles* (II.ii); and Smart begins the dedication of his verse Horace to Sir Francis Blake Delaval,

> Sir,
>   Should you ask me, what could be my inducement to under-
> take the following work at my time of day . . . I must fairly
> answer, that I made my version of Horace for the same reason, as
> he wrote the original
>
>   —Paupertas impulit audax
>   Ut versus facerem.

The important difference here is that Horace was looking back to the days of his neediness; Smart's need was great at the time that he wrote his dedication. Both men lost their paternal estate. Both relied upon patrons, the Roman poet faring much better in this respect than the English. Both were of low stature and plump, a fact to which they also allude in their poetry.

How much Smart may have been aware of these similarities is of little significance; what matters is that he felt an "affinity in the spirit" with Horace. The quoted words are from the Preface to the verse Horace and are part of Smart's opening statement to the effect that it takes more than just "deep learning and sound judgement" to translate certain of the major Latin poets. At the end of his list of these poets he places Horace: "and (above all authors and their excellencies) the lucky risk of the Horatian boldness, cannot be attempted with any success, save by men of some rank with them and affinity in the spirit." That he possessed these qualifications is attested "by the best scholars of the times both at home and abroad" and by "Mr. Pope in particular, with whom I had the honor to correspond." He continues, after a few more remarks, "As for me, I ever look'd upon Horace with extreme approbation, but never supposed him to be so wholly inimitable, that a man might not do him some degree of justice." This approbation of Horace took forms and wielded an influence on Smart's poetry other than those obviously seen in the imitations and translations discussed above. I have little doubt that, either directly, or indirectly through Prior and Pope, Smart adopted a mode of writing that went back to Horace for its ultimate inspiration.[29] That is to say, in the choice of subject, in the tone that informs his best poetry of a particular kind, and in the indefinable overall effect of a number of his poems Smart really has an "affinity in the spirit" with Horace. Certain it is that Smart absorbed many principles and techniques from Horace's precepts, chiefly in the *Art of Poetry*, as well as learning Horace's actual practice of the art of poetry.[30]

Both poets were of an amorous nature, or so their poems would have us believe, many of them being addressed to a variety of women, named, unnamed, and only partially named. Smart's amorousness, real enough I am convinced, was not, of course, modelled on Horace's, nor do I know of a love poem of Smart's deriving from a particular poem of Horace. It is more the tone of these poems to young women, facetious or semi-facetious and excellent of their kind, that is reminiscent of Horace. So it is also with Smart's "epistles," and here I refer to such poems as *To the Reverend Mr. Powell, On the non-performance of a promise he made the author of a hare*; *Epistle to Dr. Nares*; *Epistle to Mrs. Tyler*; and *An Invitation to Mrs. Tyler, A Clergyman's Lady to dine upon a couple of ducks on the anniversary of the author's wedding-day*. Their faraway models are Horace's *Satires* and *Epistles* if in nothing more than the easy colloquial tone and flair for reproducing the accents of conversation in which both poets excelled. Here is the "hare," or "non-hare," poem.

> Friend, with regard to this same Hare,
> Am I to hope, or to despair?
> By punctual Post the Letter came,
> With Powell's Hand, and Powell's Name:
> Yet there appear'd, for Love or Money,
> Nor Hare, nor Leveret, nor Coney.
> Say, my dear *Morgan*, has my Lord,
> Like other great Ones kept his Word?
> Or have you been deceiv'd by 'Squire?
> Or has your Poacher lost his Wire,
> Or in some unpropitious Hole,
> Instead of Puss, trepann'd a Mole?
> Thou valiant Son of great *Cadwallader*,
> Hast thou a Hare, or hast thou swallow'd her?
>   But now, methinks I hear you say,
> (And shake your Head) "Ah, well-a-day!
> Painful Pre-eminence to be wise,
> We WITS have such short Memories.
> Oh, that the Act was not in Force!
> A Horse!—my Kingdom for a Horse!
> To love—yet be denied the Sport!
> Oh, for a Friend or two at Court!
> God knows there's scarce a Man of Quality
> In all our peerless Principality—"
>   But hold—for on his Country joking,
> To a warm *Welchman's* most provoking,
> As for poor Puss, upon my Honour,
> I never set my Heart upon her.

26

But any Gift from Friend to Friend,
Is pleasing in its Aim and End.
I, like the Cock, wou'd spurn a Jewel,
Sent by th'unkind, th'unjust or cruel.
But honest Powell!—Sure from him
A Barley-corn wou'd be a Gem.
Pleas'd therefore had I been, and proud,
And prais'd thy generous Heart aloud,
If 'stead of Hare (but do not blab it)
You'd send me only a *Welch* Rabbit.

Smart's ability to reproduce dialogue is seen at its best in *The Midwife*; his experiences on the public stage as Mother Midnight in a series of "entertainments" of various kinds helped to sharpen his abilities in this direction. Of some slight additional interest is Smart's use of lines from Horace as epigraphs for some of his poems. All in all, the figure of the Latin poet looms large in Smart's poetic development.

Some time after the publication of his *Poems on Several Occasions* in 1752, Smart turned to his first extended preoccupation with Horace, a prose translation of his works that appeared in two duodecimo volumes in December 1755, although the edition is dated 1756. The title page makes quite clear that this is a literal translation "for the Use of those who are desirous of acquiring or recovering a competent Knowledge of the Latin Language." Need alone dictated the choice of a prose translation; Smart's brief Preface reflects the bitterness with which he undertook and carried the work to completion. Among other things he says,

> The following version being the work of a man who had made poetry, perhaps, too much the business of his life, some account of his motives for undertaking it may seem necessary. In the first place, then, there was reason to believe that a thing of this kind, properly executed, would be very useful to those who are desirous of acquiring or recovering a competent knowledge of the Latin tongue. Secondly, the extraordinary success which attempts of this kind have met with, though by men who manifestly did not understand the author, any otherwise than through a French medium, and tho' printed in large volumes, and sold at a proportionate price; gave sufficient reason for the translator to hope, that his labour would not be in vain; I say *labour*, for genius, if he had pretentions to it, could not have been exerted in the work before us.

Other statements reinforce the impression given by this apologetic opening. In keeping with the tradition that matter of dubious propriety should either be entirely cut out or at least cleaned up, Smart, with an eye to the adoption of his version as a school text, assures learned readers that he has emended some particularly offending lines.

Some idea of the quality of the work can be had by quoting the translation of one poem. The twenty-third *Ode* of the first Book, *Vitas hinnuleo me similis, Chloe*, which should be compared with Smart's verse translation (see below in this introduction), is rendered thus in the prose version:

> O Chloe, you avoid me like a fawn, that is seeking its fearful mother in the trackless mountains, not without a causeless apprehension of the breezes of the wood. For, whether the approach of spring has ruffled the trembling leaves, or the green lizards have moved the bush, she trembles both in her heart and knees. But I do not pursue you like a savage tygress, or a Getulian lion, to break your bones.—At length, cease to dangle after your mother, now you are in season for a husband.

Whatever one thinks of this one translation or, having access to the whole work, of the entire version, it had some success in Smart's lifetime, going into three editions by the time he died in 1771. More remarkable, however, is the number of editions after his death, and one still reads his 1756 prose translation of the *Satires and Epistles* in the Everyman *Horace*.

But Smart profited only to the extent of £13 for his prose translation, the other £87 of the stipulated price being given to his wife, the daughter of John Newbery, publisher of the Horace. Within three years of the publication of his prose *Horace*, Smart was confined for madness in a private home, spent a year in the lunatic ward of St. Luke's Hospital (from which he was discharged uncured), and entered his third and longest period of confinement, this time in a private madhouse. There is every reason to believe that he continued to write poetry during the four years he spent in the private madhouse; one of his poems, the *Jubilate Agno*, is known to be of that period. Strangely enough, it was in *Jubilate Agno* that Smart first claimed a talent to which he was to call attention again in his Preface to the verse Horace. In the former he writes, "For my talent is to give an impression upon words by punching, that when the reader casts his eye upon 'em, he takes up the image from the mould which I have made" (B2, l. 404); in the latter, "Impression then, is a talent or gift of Almighty God, by which a Genius is impowered to throw an emphasis upon a word or sentence in such wise, that it cannot escape any reader of sheer good sense, and true critical sagacity." Since "impression," although "possessed in a degree by every great genius," is, Smart says in this same Preface, "exceeding in our Lyric to surpass," i.e., that Horace is supremely possessed of it, he is again pointing up his own fitness for the task of translating the Latin poet. One cannot be quite sure, however, precisely what Smart meant by "impression"; one footnote in the Preface tantalizes rather than helps: "This subject of Impression is altogether a copious one and to use the words of Mr. Hurd, upon another occasion, you'd require a volume to do it justice; but Mr. Smart had not an opportunity of considering it in its latitude here" (p.xxi).

Smart left the private madhouse on January 30 or 31, 1763, and, having established himself in decent lodgings, immediately turned to the business of supporting himself by his poetry. In April his best-known poem, *A Song to David*, was published, and in the next two or three years three more slim volumes of his poetry appeared. These were followed by his verse translation of the Psalms of David and the *Hymns and Spiritual Songs for the Fasts and Festivals of the Church of England*, published together. During this same period he wrote the lyrics for *Hannah*, an oratorio with music by John Worgan, and translated the fables of Phædrus into verse. All his efforts to keep his head above water were in vain, however, for the *Song* was grossly misunderstood and severely criticized, the three volumes of poetry earned him little, *Hannah* survived only one performance, and the translation of Phædrus did not bring him much. But all or most of this time Smart was also preparing a verse translation of Horace and revising his 1756 prose translation. Our knowledge of this comes from a letter written by Dr. John Hawkesworth, a kind of literary jack-of-all-trades, who was a friend of Smart's as well as of most other literary figures of London. In October 1764 he wrote to Smart's elder sister, Mrs. Margaret Hunter, then living in Margate, of his visit to her brother:

> I perceived upon his table a quarto book, in which he had been writing, a prayer book, and a Horace. . . . I found he had compleated a translation of Phaedrus in verse for Dodsley at a certain price, and that now he is busy in translating all Horace into verse. . . . He told me his principal motive for translating Horace into verse, was to supersede the prose translation, which he did for Newbery, which he said would hurt his memory. He intends however to review that translation, and print it at the foot of the page in his poetical version, which he proposes to print in quarto with the Latin, both in verse and prose, on the opposite page.[31]

Smart was not only translating Horace into verse but was at the same time "reviewing," i.e., revising, his prose translation. While this revision is not of primary importance, I would point out that no prose translation remained untouched, the revisions extending in some cases to virtual retranslation of entire poems.[32]

A little less than three years after Hawkesworth's visit to Smart the verse Horace came out in four handsome volumes. Accompanying the verse translation, as promised on the title page, was "a prose translation, for the help of students." Included in the second volume was Smart's Cambridge translation of Pope's *Ode on Saint Cecilia's Day* in

Latin, with a prefatory note to the effect that "in order to exercise the student in the Horatian measures, and at the same time (as I trust) to give him no mean entertainment, I have subjoined my translation of Mr. Pope's Ode on St. Cecelia's day, written when I was a youth, and for which I had the honour of a very handsome letter of thanks from that celebrated Author." Volume two was also swelled by Rodellius's Latin life of Horace deriving from Suetonius's *Vita Horati*, by four pages devoted to a piece entitled *De Mæcenatis, Stirpe vere Regia*, by Rodellius's chronological synopsis in Latin of Roman history necessary for an understanding of Horace, and by a catalogue of the *Odes* arranged according to their respective Latin metres. Volume three began with Andre Dacier's Preface to Horace's *Satires*, also in Latin. All this, and some remarks in the Preface, lead to the belief that Smart hoped his version would be adopted as a textbook and hence bring him relief from his ever-present and ever-growing need. Hawkesworth had anticipated this possibility, for he wrote, in the letter quoted above, that if the translation "is not adopted as a school book, which perhaps may be the case, it will turn to little account." About three years after publication of the verse *Horace*, Smart was arrested for debt, and a year later he died in the King's Bench Prison—his translation had not been adopted.

The Preface to the verse *Horace* was more than just another traditional bit of prolegomenous matter for Smart. He seized this public occasion to relieve himself of a number of complaints that had been rankling in his breast for years: the neglect he had suffered as a poet, his lack of patronage, the pressures under which he had had to write his poetry, and the decline in his family's fortunes. He concludes:

> Good-nature is the grace of God in grain, and so much the characteristic of an Englishman, that I hope every one deserving such a name will think it somewhat hard, if a gentleman derived from ancestors, who have abode upon their own Lordship six hundred years in the County Palatine of Durham, should have been reduced in a manner by necessity to a work of this kind which if done in a state, he had more reason to be satisfied with, had been more likely to have given satisfaction.

But this same Preface allowed him to have his say upon Horace, to characterize that poet's style and manner, and to advance a novel theory of his own. Unfortunately, his discovery that the first part of Horace's *Art of Poetry* is, in his own words, "a manifest ridicule of the Metamorphoses of Ovid," a discovery upon which eight pages are lavished, is chronologically impossible. Horace had been dead for some time before Ovid began the *Metamorphoses*. Evidently others were unaware of this last fact, or at least one can so interpret the silence of the writer for the Critical Review who reviewed the translation. Although he said nothing about the Horace-Ovid theory, he had a good deal to say about Smart's diction and about the success or failure of one or another of the translations of particular poems. All in all, considering that the Critical Review had manhandled Smart more than once earlier, the translation did not fare too badly at the hands of the reviewer.[33]

Hawkesworth, when visiting Smart in late 1764, had some of the translation of Horace read to him and commented in his letter to Smart's sister that "it is very clever; and his own poetical fire sparkles in it very frequently; yet, upon the whole, it will scarcely take the place of Francis's." Hawkesworth evidently expected Margaret Hunter to have heard of Francis's Horace by virtue of its popularity and relative longevity. As I have suggested above, any translator of Horace after 1746 would have to have his eye on Francis's version. And while there is no need for readers today to judge Smart's version by eighteenth-century standards, comparison of his translation with Francis's in a few poems will reveal much about the differences that make Smart's a poetic achievement that can still be admired without apologetic allowances for the faults that stem from the period in which he wrote. In brief, Francis's is a good eighteenth-century verse translation of Horace; Smart's translation is, in most cases, good by any standards. Nor is it primarily as translations that they must be judged. Johnson was not being idiosyncratic when he told Boswell during one of the briskest conversations in the Life that "we must try its effect as an English poem; that is the way to judge of the merit of a translation. Translations are, in general, for people, who cannot read the original."[34] At about the same time he said this in conversation, Johnson was writing his life of Dryden, in which he remarked that a translator "is to exhibit his author's thoughts in such a dress of diction as the author would have given them had his language been English: rugged magnificence is not to be softened, hyperbolical ostentation is not to be repressed, nor sententious affectation to have its point blunted. A translator is to be like his author: it is not his business to excel him" (Lives, I, 423). That translation of Horace was best, then, that most faithfully recaptured those aspects of his poetry that made him unique.

Philip Francis—unsuccessful dramatist, minor political pamphleteer, clergyman, schoolmaster, and tutor to a son of the nobility— seems a strange person to have had such success as translator of Horace. His one other published translation, Demosthenes' Orations, two volumes, 1757-58, did not supersede the existing English translation and brought him no additional fame. Indeed, his sole claims to remembrance consist of the translation of Horace, his earliest work, and of the fact that he was father of the likeliest candidate for identification as Junius, the mysterious and powerful political satirist who won such notoriety with a series of letters between 1769 and 1772. Little in the elder Francis's life bespeaks that "affinity in the spirit" which Smart saw as a link between himself and Horace. And yet in spite of that handicap Francis seems to have hit upon the kind of verse translation of Horace that his contemporaries wanted; Smart did not.

Smart's career as a poet divides rather conveniently into two periods marked by the four-year stay in the private madhouse. Before his admission into the madhouse he tried his hand at a number of different kinds of poetry; during his confinement and after leaving it most of his poetry was religious. His best poetry in the years up to this confinement was that in which he addressed one of a number of young women in a vein of half-humorous, half-serious gallantry, or in which he adopted the urbane manner of a man of the world engaged in conversation with others whose predilections were like his own. Much of what he wrote in this period was of an occasional nature, thrown off quickly and later published without revision—for he was not one to waste a poem even if it was written for a private or domestic occasion. Although this easy, familiar tone occurs in only a very few poems between 1763 and 1767, the period from his release from confinement to the publication of the verse *Horace*, it emerged prominently in his translation and marked his best efforts. Where his own temperament or poetic bent most closely resembled Horace's, there he achieved his best effects.

Horace's *To Lydia*, the eighth *Ode* of the first Book, is a lyric in which the poet "animadverts upon Sybaris, a youth distractedly in love with Lydia, and wholly dissolved in pleasures," a subject to which Smart could do ample justice.

> I charge thee, Lydia, tell me straight,
>   Why Sybaris destroy,
> Why make love do the deeds of hate,
> And to his end precipitate
>   The dear enamour'd boy?
> Why can he not the field abide,
>   From sun and dust recede,
> Nor with his friends, in gallant pride,
> Dress'd in his regimentals, ride,
>   And curb the manag'd steed?
> Why does he now to bathe disdain,
>   And fear the sandy flood?
> Why from th'athletic oil refrain,
> As if its use would be his bane,
>   As sure as viper's blood?
> No more his shoulders black and blue
>   By wearing arms appear;
> He, who the quoit so dextrous threw,

> And from whose hand the jav'lin flew
> > Beyond a rival's spear;
> Why does he skulk, as authors say
> > Of Thetis' fav'rite heir,
> Lest a man's habit should betray,
> And force him to his troops away,
> > The work of death to share?

In "dear enamour'd boy," from Horace's "amando," and in "Nor with his friends, in gallant pride,/ Dress'd in his regimentals, ride," from Horace's "Cur neque militaris/ Inter æquales equitet?" something of the quality of Smart's characteristic idiom in this translation of Horace's works emerges. Sybaris is no remote figure from the pages of an old book; he is a contemporary young officer in love with a somewhat coquettish young lady who has so distracted him that he forbears to go riding in his regimentals—a gratuitous and happy touch—with his fellows. Francis calls Sybaris a "too amorous Boy" and asks "Or why no more with martial Pride,/ Amidst the youthful Battel ride," closer to Horace in this last than Smart with his "regimentals."

The differences between Smart's version and Francis's can be further seen by comparison of their translations of Book. I, *Ode* xxiii, another poem in which Smart might be expected to appear to best advantage. Francis translates:

> Chloe flies me like a Fawn,
> Which through some sequester'd Lawn
> Panting seeks the Mother-Deer,
> Not without a panic Fear
> Of the gently-breathing Breeze,
> And the Motion of the Trees.
> If the curling Leaves but shake,
> If a Lizard stir the Brake,
> Frighted it begins to freeze,
> Trembling both at Heart and Knees.
> But not like a Tyger dire,
> Nor a Lion, fraught with Ire,
> I pursue my lovely Game,
> To destroy thy tender Frame.
> Haste thee, leave thy Mother's Arms,
> Ripe for Love are all thy Charms.

Smart's translation reads:

> Me, Chloe, like a fawn you fly,
> That seeks in trackless mountains high
> > Her tim'rous dam again;
> Alarm'd at every thing she hears,

> The woods, the winds excite her fears,
>   Tho' all those fears are vain.
> For if a tree the breeze receives,
> That plays upon the quiv'ring leaves
>   When spring begins to start;
> Or if green lizards, where they hide,
> Turn but the budding bush aside,
>   She trembles knees and heart.
> But I continue my pursuit,
> Not like the fierce Getulian brute,
>   Or tyger, to assail,
> And of thee life and limbs bereave—
> Think now at last 'tis time to leave
>   Thy mother for a male.

At times, both in this poem and in others, Smart is more literal, at other times Francis is. But where Francis rejects Horace's "montibus aviis" for the rather pretty and familiar—even traditional—"sequester'd Lawn," Smart is satisfied with a very literal "trackless mountain." His "She trembles knees and heart" adopts Horace's Latin construction, "Et corde et genibus tremit," doing away with any preposition, a piece of daring of which Francis is incapable. Francis's "tender frame" becomes in Smart "life and limbs," both one of his alliterative doublets and at the same time a more concrete phrase than the again unsurprising one chosen by his predecessor. Finally, for the last line of a poem is so strategically important especially in a poem of this kind, Smart stays with Horace in his "think now at last 'tis time to leave/ Thy mother for a male," when all that Francis can rise to is "Haste thee, leave thy Mother's Arms,/ Ripe for Love are all thy Charms." Francis is too polite here, "love" is too delicate a euphemism for Horace's "viro"; Smart's "male" begs no question.

Smart's early imitations of Horace affected his later translation of many of the poems. His manner was already fixed in some degree, and where, in the imitation, he could allow himself great latitude, in the translation he limited himself somewhat but still took certain freedoms which derive ultimately from those same translations. The imitation of *To Lyce*, written about 1750 and included earlier in this introduction, substitutes modern names for those of Horace's contemporaries and adds details rather liberally.[35] The translation, however, actually improves upon the colloquial, conversational tone of the imitation:

> Lyce, the gods my vows have heard,
>   At length they've heard my vows;
> You wou'd be beauteous with a beard,
>   You romp and you carouse:
> And drunk, with trembling voice, you court
>   Slow Cupid, prone to seek

For better music, bloom, and sport,
  In buxom Chia's cheek.
For he, a sauce-box, scorns dry chips,
  And teeth decay'd and green;
Where wrinkled forehead, and chapt lips,
  And snowy hairs are seen.
Nor Coan elegance, nor gems,
  Your past years will restore;
Which time to his records condemns,
  With fleeting wings of yore.
Ah! where's that form, complexion, grace,
  That air—where is she, say,
That cou'd my sick'ning soul solace,
  And stole my heart away?
Blest! who cou'd Cynara succeed,
  As artful and as fair—
But fate, to Cynara, decreed
  Few summers for her share,
That crow-like Lyce might survive,
  'Till lads shou'd laugh and shout,
To see the torch, but just alive,
  So slowly stinking out.

For the most part, the translation is less poetic in the sense that there
are no "sapless and bare" tree trunks and no "pliant young Branches"
but rather "dry chips." Nor does Mother Gunter sport a beard,
whereas Lyce is given one, without any warrant in Horace's text for
such an addition. And while the poem on Mother Gunter ends with
the reminder that "Love hot as fire must be burnt to a coal,/ As the
Broomstick concludes in an Ember," the lads of the poem to Lyce
laugh and shout "To see the torch, but just alive,/ So slowly stinking
out," a more fitting end for "an antiquated courtezan" (Smart's translation of Horace's "meretricem vetulam") whose "teeth decay'd and
green" and "chapt lips" would insure a bad breath. Francis does not
endow Lyce with a beard; and for him Cynara "died in beauty's
bloom" where Smart has fate decree her "few summers for her share."
Smart's "crow-like Lyce" is "the raven's rival" in Francis, and the
latter's version ends more literally, but much less memorably, as the
torch spreads a "sickly Gleam" and expires "in a Smoke."
  Smart's imitation of the fourth *Ode* of the second Book, *Ad Xanthi-
am Phoceum*, which he called *The Pretty Chambermaid* (included earlier
in this introduction), expands on its original and introduces matter not
to be found there.[36] But the translation stays within the bounds of the
original, both in number of lines and content, with of course certain li-
berties of expression:

O Phoceus, think it no disgrace
To love your maid, since Thetis heir,
Tho' proud, of old was in your case,
    Briseis was so fair,
The slave Tecmessa at her feet
Saw her lord Ajax—Atreus son
Lov'd his fair captive in the heat
    Of conquest, that he won,
When beat by that Thessalian boy,
The Phrygian host was disarray'd,
And Hector's death, the fall of Troy,
    An easy purchase made.
Who knows what wealth thou hast to claim,
Rich parents may thy Phyllis grace,
Surely the Gods have been to blame
    To one of royal race.
You cannot think her meanly born,
Nor worthless could her mother be,
Whose heart has such ingenuous scorn
    For wealth, and love for thee.
Her face, her limbs so form'd t'engage,
I praise with a safe conscience still—
Shun to suspect a man, whose age
    Is going down the hill.

Again Francis's version of this same *Ode* points up those aspects of the two translations that were evidently responsible for the greater popularity of his work.

Blush not, my Phoceus, though a Dame
Of servile State thy Breast enflame;
A Slave could stern Achilles move,
And bend his haughty Soul to Love;
Ajax, invincible in Arms,
Was captiv'd by his Captive's Charms:
Atrides, midst his Triumphs mourn'd,
And for a ravished Virgin burn'd,
What Time, the fierce Barbarian Bands
Fell by Peleides' conquering Hands,
And Troy (her Hector swept away)
Became to Greece an easier Prey.
Who knows, when Phillis is your Bride,
To what fine Folk you'll be allied;
Her Parents dear, of gentle Race,
Shall not their Son-in-law disgrace.
She sprung from Kings, or nothing less.
And weeps the Family's Distress.
Think not that such a charming She,
Can of the sordid Vulgar be;

> To shameless, prostituted Earth,
> Think not that Phillis owes her Birth,
> Who with such Firmness could disdain.
> The Force and Flatteries of Gain.
> Yet after all, believe me, Friend,
> I can with Innocence commend
> Her blooming Face, her snowy Arms,
> Her taper Leg, and all her Charms,
> For, trembling on to forty Years,
> My Age forbids all jealous Fears.

Francis's "Fell by Peleides' conquering Hands" suffers a sea change to become "When beat by that Thessalian boy" in Smart's version, and where the latter again falls into the language of the young man about London in "An easy purchase made" Francis has "Become to Greece an easier Prey." One way in which Smart consciously strove to emulate the urbane Roman was by using the current modes of speech of polite and impolite London society. He had shown, certainly as early as *The Midwife*, that his ear was attuned to the give and take of coffee-house conversation; he improved in his ability to reproduce such conversation in the material he wrote for Mrs. Midnight's entertainments; and he had lost none of it when he came to translate Horace. One has only to turn to his translation of the *Epistles* and *Satires*, especially the sixth Satire of the second Book, to see this quality of his art in operation.

One final aspect of Smart's translation needs exploration. He had remarked in a note in the *Universal Visiter* (1756, p. 9) that Pope's St. Cecilia's Day ode contained some thirty different metres, a fact to which he again referred in the verse *Horace* itself. Throughout his career as a poet Smart had experimented with a number of metrical and stanzaic patterns, nowhere with greater virtuosity than in his version of the Psalms with the accompanying *Hymns and Spiritual Songs for the Fasts and Festivals of the Church of England*. Indeed, as an exercise and a flourish, Smart rendered the *Gloria Patri* into twenty-five different measures and appended the poems to the Psalms as a specimen of the measures employed in the foregoing work. Sometimes, in the Psalms, he would write his version of a particular Psalm in one stanzaic form and then, for no stated reason, add another version in a different form. He was ever conscious of the music of verse and of the affinity of music and language. One passage in *Jubilate Agno* exemplifies this preoccupation perfectly.

> For the trumpet rhimes are sound bound,
> soar more and the like.
> For the Shawm rhimes are lawn fawn
> moon boon and the like.
> For the harp rhimes are sing ring,
> string & the like.

>For the cymbal rhimes are bell well
>>toll soul & the like.
>For the flute rhimes are tooth youth
>>suit mute & the like.
>For the dulcimer rhimes are grace place
>>beat heat & the like.
>For the Clarinet rhimes are clean
>>seen and the like.
>For the Bassoon rhimes are pass, class and the like.
>>God be gracious to Baumgarden.
>For the dulcimer are rather van fan &
>>the like and grace place &c are of the bassoon.
>For beat heat, weep peep &c are of the pipe.
>For every word has its marrow in the English tongue
>>for order and for delight.[37]

Smart, it may be well to recall, moved in musical circles and more than once in his poetry showed that he took a keen delight in music.

Included in the scholarly apparatus in the verse Horace was, as I have already mentioned, an analysis of all the *Odes* broken down into the twenty-two Latin metres in which they were written. Revealed as the favorite metre was one which resulted in translation in a stanza made up of two iambic lines of eight syllables, one of ten, and one of twelve, rhyming *a a b b.* Here as an example is Book I, *Ode* xxvii, in Smart's translation.

>With glasses form'd for joy to fight,
>Is what the Thracians do in spite;
>Let Bacchus know no barb'rous customs here,
>But keep the modest God from bloody discord clear.
>>Can such strange contraries agree,
>>As wine and lights in social glee,
>And sabres such as savage Media wears—
>Cease your vile noise, my friends, nor quit your easy chairs.
>>Me too!—shall I your revels join,
>>And sour my good Falernian wine?
>No, let the brother of the Locrian fair,
>Rather his lovesick joys, and darling flame declare.
>>He will not—On no other plan,
>>No other terms I take my can—
>Whatever damsel e'er thy breast inflam'd,
>Was of ingenuous birth, nor need you be ashamed.
>>Whatever be the case speak out
>>To friendly ears, nor make a doubt.—
>"Ah, wretch! how thou art hamper'd in a straight,
>"A lad whose matchless worth deserv'd a better fate."
>>What sorceress, what magic art,
>>What pow'r divine can ease thy smart?—

> E'en Pegasus to clear thee will be loth
> From one compos'd of whimsy, wantonness and wrath.

When Smart came to the thirty-eighth *Ode* of the first Book he noted under the title of that poem, "In the original metre exactly." The resulting translation, a bit of pyrotechnics with the demanding Sapphics, sounds like a poem of the mid-nineteenth century, something Smart's admirer, Robert Browning, might have written.

> Persian pomps, boy, ever I renounce them:
> Scoff o' the plaited coronet's refulgence;
> Seek not in fruitless vigilance the rose-tree's
>   Tardier offspring.
>
> Mere honest myrtle that alone is order'd,
> Me the mere myrtle decorates, as also
> Thee the prompt waiter to a jolly toper
>   Hous'd in an arbour.

Elsewhere Smart calls attention again to his practice of imitating the original meter as closely as possible.[38] He was doubtless proud of his abilities; he was also pushing into greater prominence an aspect of his work designed to attract prospective buyers.

Within three years of the date of publication of the verse *Horace* Smart was in the King's Bench Prison as a debtor. He died after a little more than a year of confinement there. His hopes of redeeming himself by the successful sale of the Horace as a text for students had been bitterly disappointed. For the last four years of his life he was unable to produce poetry of any excellence except in some of the hymns in his last published work, *Hymns for the Amusement of Children*; the rest was hack work. He died without ever having been accorded the full measure of recognition as a poet that he deserved. But the works that his contemporaries could not appreciate, his greatest poems—*A Song of David*, the Psalms, the *Hymns and Spiritual Songs for the Fasts and Festivals of the Church of England*—and the verse translation of Horace, although belatedly for this last, have finally come into their own.

The 1767 edition is somewhat carelessly printed. Page numbers and even the numbering of odes sometimes contain mistakes, and the text has a fair number of printers' errors, such as "Pagasus," "Promotheus," "Menerva," "brids" (for "birds"), "distiny" (for "destiny"). These, when obvious, have been silently corrected. Generally, however, the text below follows the "accidentals" of *1767* (with the exception, of course, of the long *s*). Old variant spellings such as "houshold," "desart," "woful," and "atchieve," which cannot mislead the reader, have been retained. A few which may be a little puzzling perhaps need explanation: "drougth" (III. iv) for modern "drought" or "drouth"; "cag" (III. xv) for "keg"; "casoons" (III. xxiv) for "caissons." "Fort" (I. xiv and III. xxvii) could easily be a compositor's mistake for "sort" (from *sors,* fate), which would be a satisfactory rendering of the Latin in both instances. But "fort" ("forte" in modern spelling), often found in the metaphor from fencing, "fort and foible,"—see the *O.E.D.*—seems to have been popular at the time, and in the second occurrence it forms part of an alliterative doublet, something Smart was fond of. One substantive emendation has been made—in I. vii, line 34, "please" for the text's "pleases," which would spoil the rhyme and is no doubt the work of the compositor. In accordance with the practice of the time (see the "Grammar" prefaced to Johnson's *Dictionary*), plural possessives in the text have no apostrophes; these have been supplied. Smart's version omits what is now listed as *Ode* X of Book IV, "O crudelis adhuc et Veneris muneribus potens," and his numbering of the subsequent odes is one less than in modern editions.

Notes to Introduction

[1]Translated from Bentley's Latin Preface by R. C. Jebb, from whose *Bentley* (New York, 1882), p. 123, I quote.

[2]See Caroline Goad, *Horace in the English Literature of the Eighteenth Century* (New Haven, 1918) and Chapter 2, "Horace and the Eighteenth Century," in R. M. Ogilvie, *Latin and Greek, A History of the Influence of the Classics on English Life from 1600 to 1918* (Hamden, Conn., 1964) for a detailed analysis of Horace's influence.

[3]Quoted in Ogilvie, *Latin and Greek*, p. 45.

[4]See Maynard Mack, *"Secretum Iter:* Some Uses of Retirement Literature in the Poetry of Pope," in *Aspects of the Eighteenth Century,* ed. Earl Wasserman (Baltimore, 1965), pp. 207-243 for some influences other than Horace's.

[5]*Alexander Pope, The Poetry of Allusion* (Oxford, 1959), pp. 163 and 164-65.

[6]*Latin and Greek,* pp. 47-50. See Howard D. Weinbrot, *Augustus Caesar in "Augustan England": The Decline of a Classical Norm* (Princeton, 1978) for a contrary view.

[7]*Lives of the Poets,* ed. G. B. Hill (Oxford, 1905), III, 176 and 246-47. Johnson's view has been recently criticized by Aubrey Williams in his "Pope and Horace: *The Second Epistle of the Second Book,"* Restoration and Eighteenth-Century Literature, Essays in Honor of Alan Dugald McKillop, ed. by Carroll Camden (Chicago, 1963), pp. 309-21.

[8]*Essays,* ed. W. P. Ker (Oxford, 1900), I, 237-239.

[9]I quote the Loeb translation; Cowley's poem is in his *Miscellanies.* Sir Ronald Storrs, in *Ad Pyrrham, A Polyglot Collection of Translations* (Oxford, 1959), reprints over a hundred versions of this ode. By 1959 the polyglot collection numbered 451 versions. See below, p. 50 for Smart's translation.

[10]See Harold F. Brooks, "The 'Imitation' in English Poetry, Especially in Formal Satire, Before the Age of Pope," *Review of English Studies*, XXV (1949), 124-40. Sprat's poem appears in *Poems by Horace*, ed. Alexander Brome, 1666.

[11]See my *New Essays by Arthur Murphy* (East Lansing, 1963), pp. 5-6.

[12]Three from the *Satires*, two from the *Art of Poetry*, and one each from the *Odes*, *Epistles*, and *Carmen Seculare*. But he is cited 103 times in the 208 *Ramblers*.

[13]*Life of Samuel Johnson*, ed. Hill-Powell (Oxford, 1934-50), I, 70 and *Lives of the English Poets*, ed. G. B. Hill (Oxford, 1905), I, 447. Hereafter *Life* and *Lives*. John Butt, "Johnson and the Poetical Imitation," in *New Light on Dr. Johnson*, ed. F. W. Hilles (New Haven, 1959), pp. 24 and 25, points out that Johnson, newly arrived in the city and without friends, could not have taken Horace for his model; he had to adopt Juvenal's stance. See, however, Patrick O'Flaherty in *ELH*, XXXIV (1967), 78-91 for a contrary view.

[14]*The Correspondence of Alexander Pope*, ed. George Sherburn (Oxford, 1956), III, 37.

[15]See, however, Brower, *Alexander Pope*, p. 281, where Pope in the *Epistle to a Lady* "is philosophic in Horace's most characteristic manner. . . . It is Horatian too in Pope's refusal to be dazzled by social prestige or pretension to wisdom, and in his quiet testimony to deep but free and easy friendship."

[16]A reviewer for the *Monthly Review*, XVIII (1758), 45, writes of the difficulty of translating Horace and glances at Creech: "Accordingly we find, that an eminent poet of the last century, who had done ample justice to the philosophical Lucretius, lost all his laurels by an essay of this kind." Yet Dryden praised Creech's translation in his Preface to *Cleomenes*.

[17]See John Butt, ed. *Imitations of Horace*, vol. IV of the Twickenham *Pope* (London, 1939), p. xliii, n. 5.

[18]*Essays*, ed. Ker, I, 241.

[19]*Essays*, ed. Ker, I, 254.

[20]George Watson, ed., *John Dryden, "Of Dramatic Poesy" And Other Critical Essays* (Everyman ed., 1962), II, 31, n. 1, suggests that "numerousness" is "Probably a unique usage, meaning metrical perfections."

[21]*Essays*, ed. Ker, I, 266-67.

[22]Jebb, *Bentley*, p. 123.

[23]Ogilvie, *Latin and Greek*, p. 46 lists a number of other editions, intermingled with translations, that appeared before and after Bentley's.

[24]See James Henry Monk, *The Life of Richard Bentley, D.D.*, 2n ed. (London, 1833), I, 316-19, for this and other attacks on Bentley. For identification of Oldisworth, see *Richard Bentley, D.D. A Bibliography of his Works and of all the Literature called Forth by his Acts or Writing*, compiled by A. T. Bartholomew and J. W. Clark (Cambridge, 1908), p. 49.

[25]Monk, *Bentley*, II, 413.

41

[26]Christopher Hunter, ed., *Poems of the Late Christopher Smart*, 2 vols. (Reading, 1791).

[27]See Robert Brittain, ed. *Poems by Christopher Smart* (Princeton, 1950), p. 9, n.7 for some of these.

[28]See, among others, *Odes* I. ii and x.

[29]Hunter finds "the grace and ease of Prior" in Smart's fables (p. xxxviii). See also my "Survival in Grub-Street. . .," *Bulletin of the New York Public Library*, 64 (1960), p. 149, n.6, for laudatory references to Prior in Smart's poetry.

[30]See Brittain, *Poems by Christopher Smart*, pp. 67-73, for an excellent discussion of Smart and Horace. I am inclined to see more affinity between the two poets than Dr. Brittain does.

[31]Quoted in Hunter, pp. xxiii and xxiv.

[32]See my "Christopher Smart's Three Translations of Horace," *Journal of English and Germanic Philology*, LXVI (1967), 347-58, on these revisions and their effects on the verse translation.

[33]August, 1767, XXIV, 94-105.

[34]III, 256. Compare Sir Ronald Storrs, *Ad Pyrrham*, p. 26, on Milton's translation of that poem (*Odes*, I. v): "Milton's might be the best translation if it were not intelligible only to readers so steeped in accurate knowledge of the original as to have no need of it."

[35]Quoted above, pp. 21-2. The original is *Odes*, IV, xii in Smart's numbering.

[36]Quoted above, pp. 23-4.

[37]B2, 587-597 in William Bond's ed., 1954.

[38]See his remarks on *Odes* xi and xviii of the first Book, pp. 57 and 66 below.

Different men have their several pleasures: Horace affects the name of
a poet, especially in the lyric cast.

Mæcenas, of a race renown'd,
Whose royal ancestors were crown'd;
O patron of my wealth and praise,
And pride and pleasure of my days!
Some of a vent'rous cast there are,
That glory in th'Olympic car,
Whose glowing wheels in dust they roll,
Driv'n to an inch upon the goal,
And rise from mortal to divine,
Ennobled by the wreath they twine.
One, if the giddy mob proclaim,
And vying lift to * threefold fame;
One, if within his barn he stores
The wealth of Lybian threshing-floors,
Will never from his course be press'd,
For all that Attalus possess'd,
To plow, with sailor's anxious pain,
In Cyprian sloop th'Egean main.
The merchant, dreading the south-west,
Whose blasts th'Icarian wave molest,
Praises his villa's rural ease,
Built amongst bowling-greens and trees;
But soon the thoughts of growing poor
Make him his shatter'd barks insure.
There's now and then a social soul
That will not scorn the Massic bowl,
Nor shuns to break in a degree
On the grave day's solidity;
Now underneath the shrubby shade,
Now by the sacred fountain laid.

43

Many are for the martial strife,
And love the trumpet and the fife,
That mingle in the din of war,
Which all the pious dames abhor:
The sportsman, heedless of his fair,
With patience braves the wintry air,
Whether his blood-hounds, staunch and keen,
The hind have in the covert seen,
Or wild boar of the Marsian breed,
From the round-twisted cords is freed.
But as for Horace, I espouse
The glory of the scholar's brows,
The wreath of festive ivy wove,
Which makes one company for Jove.
Me the cool groves by zephyrs fann'd,
Where nymphs and satyrs, hand in hand,
Dance nimbly to the rural song,
Distinguish from the vulgar throng.
If nor Euterpe, heavenly gay,
Forbid her pleasant pipes to play,
Nor Polyhymnia disdain
A lesson in the Lesbian strain,
That, thro' Mæcenas, I may pass
'Mongst writers of the Lyric class,
My muse her laurell'd head shall rear,
And top the zenith of her sphere.

*To the three greatest honours of Rome; to be either ediles, prætors, or consuls.

Many storms and tempests are inflicted upon the Roman people, to avenge the death of Julius Cæsar. The sole hope of the empire is placed in the safety of Augustus.

Surely at length it may suffice,
These frequent storms of snow and hail,
Which Jove, commission'd from the skies,
    So dreadful to prevail!
And hurling from his flaming arm
His vengeful bolts, 'midst thunder-show'rs
Has o'er the city spread th'alarm,
    And smote the sacred tow'rs.
Thro' all the world th'alarm is spread,
For fear of those portentous days,
When Proteus on the mountain's head
    Made his sea-monsters graze.
On topmost elms the scaly race
Stuck where the ring-doves us'd to be,
And tim'rous deer, expell'd their place,
    Swam in the whelming sea.
We saw the sandy Tiber drive
Huge billows from th'Etrurian strand,
And e'en at Vesta's fane arrive
    To mar, what Numa plann'd.
Whilst vengeful 'gainst the will supreme
He fondling hears * his wife complain,
And flooding to the left his stream,
    He glories in our bane.
Thinn'd by our crimes our sons shall tell,
How Romans whet the sword and spear,
(Against the Persians had been well)
    And all our broils shall hear.
What pow'r to save her sinking name
Shall Rome invoke, what urgent suit
Shall Vesta's holy virgin's frame
    In hymns that bear no fruit.
What worthy, for the nation's aid,
Our crimes t'atone shall Jove assign,
Come white-rob'd Phœbus, as we've pray'd,
    Do thou thyself divine?

Or if thou rather wouldst befriend
Glad queen of Eryce's perfumes,
Whom love and pleasantry attend
    With their ambrosial plumes—
Or, Mars, if thou at length wouldst speed,
O founder of the Roman race,
To visit thy neglected seed,
    Now sunk into disgrace:
Too long indulg'd thy cruel sport,
Whom noise, and polish'd helms delight,
And the fierce Moor's determin'd port,
    And aspect in the fight.
Or if the part you can sustain,
By thee the righteous deed be done,
You, † which yourself a mortal feign,
    O gentle Maia's son:
Late may'st thou be again receiv'd,
And long in gladness rule our state,
Nor thee at all our vices griev'd,
    Th'unwelcome gale translate!
Here rather be the triumph priz'd,
And, father, emp'ror dear to Rome,
Delight thine ear——nor unchastis'd,
    Let scamp'ring Medes presume!

*Ilia, the mother of Romulus, was cast into the Tiber; and hence (as some will
have it) poetically called his wife. It is likely she was very fond to walk by that
pleasant river, till she was wedded to the place.

† The poet here supposes Augustus to be Mercury, in a human shape. There are
many reasons (says Rodellius) wherefore Augustus might be likened to Mercury:
for if the courier in ordinary of the Gods was expert in business, quick, and
resembling a lively youth, Octavius, the minister of providence for the repose of
mankind, was all this also, at that time being twenty-three. Mercury was the
God of genius and address, Octavius a very great patron of the one, and a most
consummate master of the other.

ODE III.

He prays that the ship may have a good passage, which was about to carry Virgil to Athens: after which he, with great spirit inveighs against the temerity of mankind.

So may the queen of Cyprus' isle
And Helen's brethren in sweet star-light smile,
  And Æolus the winds arrest,
All but the fav'ring gales of fresh north-west,
  O ship, that ow'st so great a debt,
No less than * Virgil, to our fond regret!
  By thee on yon Athenian shore
Let him be safely landed, I implore:
  And o'er the billows, as they roll,
Preserve the larger portion of my soul!
  A heart of oak, and breast of brass
Were his, who first presum'd on seas to pass,
  And ever ventur'd to engage,
In a slight skiff, with ocean's desperate rage;
  Nor fear'd to hear the cracking masts,
When Africus contends with northern blasts;
  Nor Hyads, still foreboding storms,
Nor wrathful south, that all the depth deforms;
  Than whom no greater tyrant reigns
Whether the waves he ruffles or restrains.
  How dauntless of all death was he,
Whose tearless eyes could such strange monsters see;
  Cou'd see the swelling ocean low'r,
Or those huge rocks, which in Epirus tow'r!
  Dread Providence the land in vain
Has cut from that dissociable main,
  If impious mortals not the less
On this forbidden element transgress:
  Determin'd each extreme to bear,
All desp'rate deeds the race of mortals dare.

47

Prometheus, with presumptuous fraud,
Stole fire from heav'n, and spread the flame abroad,
  Of which dire sacrilege the fruit,
The lank consumption, and a new recruit
  Of fevers came upon mankind,
And for a long delay at first design'd,
  The last extremity advanc'd,
And urg'd the march of death, and all his pangs inhanc'd,
  With wings, not giv'n a man below,
Did Dedalus attempt in air to go.
  Th'Herculean toil, exceeding bound,
Broke through the gulf of Acheron profound.
  Nothing too difficult for man,
He'll scale the skies in folly, if he can;
  Nor by his vices every day
Will give Jove leave his wrathful bolts to stay.

TO SEXTIUS, A PERSON OF CONSULAR DIGNITY.*

By describing the delightfulness of spring, and urging the common lot of mortality, he exhorts Sextius, as an Epicurean, to a life of voluptuousness.

A grateful change! Favonius, and the spring
   To the sharp winter's keener blasts succeed,
Along the beach, with ropes, the ships they bring,
   And launch again, their watry way to speed.
No more the plowmen in their cots delight,
   Nor cattle are contented in the stall;
No more the fields with hoary frosts are white,
   But Cytherean Venus leads the ball.
She, while the moon attends upon the scene,
   The Nymphs and decent Graces in the set,
Shakes with alternate feet the shaven green,
   While Vulcan's Cyclops at the anvil sweat.
Now we with myrtle shou'd adorn our brows,
   Or any flow'r that decks the loosen'd sod;
In shady groves to Faunus pay our vows,
   Whether a lamb or kid delight the God.
Pale death alike knocks at the poor man's door,
   O happy Sextius, and the royal dome,
The whole of life forbids our hope to soar,
   Death and the shades anon shall press thee home.
And when into the shallow grave you run,
   You cannot win the monarchy of wine,
Nor doat on Lycidas, as on a son,
   Whom for their spouse all little maids design.

Though this Sextius always had favoured his friend Brutus, and even at this time respected his memory, insomuch as to preserve busts of him in his house, yet Augustus, in love with such fidelity, not without prodigious applause for his generosity, chose him his colleague, in the year of Rome 713, from whence, I conjecture, (says Rodellius) that this Ode was written the year following, there being no reason to call Sextius happy before his consulate, and the season of the consulate itself not being for indulging the genius in matter of festivity.

Horace has escaped from the allurements of Pyrrha, as from a ship-
wreck. He affirms such as are ensnared by her love to be in a state of
wretchedness.

Say what slim youth, with moist perfumes
  Bedaub'd, now courts thy fond embrace,
There, where the frequent rose-tree blooms,
  And makes the grot so sweet a place?
Pyrrha, for whom with such an air
Do you bind back your golden hair?

So seeming in your cleanly vest,
  Whose plainness is the pink of taste —
Alas! how oft shall he protest
  Against his confidence misplac't,
And love's inconstant pow'rs deplore,
And wondrous winds, which, as they roar,

Throw black upon the alter'd scene —
  Who now so well himself deceives,
And thee all sunshine, all serene
  For want of better skill believes,
And for his pleasure has presag'd
Thee ever dear and disengag'd.

Wretched are all within thy snares,
  The inexperienc'd and the young!
For me the temple witness bears
  Where I my dropping weeds have hung,
And left my votive chart behind
To him that rules both wave and wind.

Varius, the tragic and epic poet, will with more address sing the atchievements of Agrippa. Horace is only fit to celebrate revels, and take pictures from middle life.

Brave and victorious in the fight,
Our Varius with Mæonian flight
   Shall thine atchievements blaze,
Whate'er, beneath thy great command,
The troops have done by sea and land,
   In fierce desire of praise.

Agrippa, I cannot attain
The grandeur of the epic strain,
   Tho' rous'd by deeds like thine,
Nor colour up the glowing page
With Peleus son's immortal rage,
   Nor reach the great design

That artful hero to recount,
Who could by sea such toils surmount;
   Nor sing the barbrous race
Of Pelops, while the bashful lyre
Thy praise and Cæsar's on the wire
   Forbids me to disgrace.

What mortal pen can Mars recite,
In adamantine armour bright,
   Or with the life compare
Meriones in dust involv'd,
Or him, Minerva's aid resolved
   The Gods themselves to dare?

I sing of sports and am'rous play,
(For all these things are in my way)
   And nymphs of sportive veins,
That are so apt to scratch and tear
With nails which to the quick they pare
   Against their fav'rite swains.

Some writers praise one city or region, and some another. Horace prefers Tibur to all the world, in which place Plancus was born, whom he exhorts to the washing away of care by wine.

Let others sing the praise of famous Rhodes
    Or Mytilene, or th'Ephesian pride,
Or chant the walls of Corinth in their odes,
    Wash'd by a different sea on either side,
Or Thebes for Bacchus, Delphi justly fam'd
    For Phœbus, or Thessalian Tempe's vale;
Some make the seat of Pallas, nymph unblam'd,
    The theme of one uninterrupted tale,
And run all lengths to wear an olive-crown—
    Many for Juno, with poetic zeal,
Argus so apt for cavalry renown,
    And, rich Mycenæ, boast thy public weal.
With me nor patient Sparta, nor the plains
    Of high-manur'd Larissa e'er cou'd take,
As where Albunea's tinkling fount remains,
    Or Anio roaring down into the lake.
And old Tiburnus' grove for ever green,
    Where flow'ring orchards give a strong perfume,
Where marshal'd trees upon the stream are seen,
    And in the waggling waters wave their bloom.
As the white south at times serenes the skies,
    Nor are his gathring show'rs for ever rife;
So thou, O Plancus, 'gainst thy cares be wise,
    With mellow wine dismiss the toils of life,
Whether the camp, with shining standards gay,
    Detain you ready for the hour of fight,
Or in your native Tibur you shall stay,
    And in the dense embow'ring shades delight.
When Teucer by his father was oppress'd,
    And driv'n away from Salamis he fled,
He thus his weeping company address'd,
    As, wet with wine, the poplar bound his head.

"Sped on by fortune, kinder than my sire,
  "O my co-mates, we'll go where'er she please;
"Despair of nothing and to all aspire—
  "By Teucer's guidance Teucer's auspices.
"For Phœbus has of certainty foretold,
  "That in a land to us advent'rers new,
"Fair Salamis a doubtful name shall hold,
  "O brave companions, O my faithful few!
"Ye that with me have harder things endur'd,
  "Than all the evils which ye now sustain,
"This day your grief and care with wine be cur'd,
  "To-morrow sends us to the depth again."

*Munatius Plancus, upon the death of Cæsar, at first sided with Octavius, and was consul with M. Lepidus, in the year of Rome, 712. After that he went over to Antony, and did not return to Augustus till 722, who, in consideration of what was past, perhaps not putting any great confidence in him, made no use of him in the war, which that very year was denounced against Antony and Cleopatra. Plancus upon this, being in a state of chagrin, stood in need of that consolation which Horace endeavours to give him in this ode.

He animadverts upon Sybaris, a youth distractedly in love with Lydia,
and wholly dissolved in pleasures.

I charge thee, Lydia, tell me straight,
   Why Sybaris destroy,
Why make love do the deeds of hate,
And to this end precipitate
   The dear enamour'd boy?
Why can he not the field abide,
   From sun and dust recede,
Nor with his friends, in gallant pride,
Dress'd in his regimentals, ride,
   And curb the manag'd steed?
Why does he now to bathe disdain,
   And fear the sandy flood?
Why from th'athletic oil refrain,
As if its use would be his bane,
   As sure as viper's blood?
No more his shoulders black and blue
   By wearing arms appear;
He, who the quoit so dextrous threw,
And from whose hand the jav'lin flew
   Beyond a rival's spear;
Why does he skulk, as authors say
   Of Thetis' fav'rite heir,
Lest a man's habit should betray,
And force him to his troops away,
   The work of death to share?

The greater the violence of the winter, the more we should indulge in festivity.

See high Soracte, white with snow,
    Still more and more a mountain grow,
Nor can the lab'ring woods their weight sustain,
And motionless with frost the sharpen'd streams remain.
    Dissolve the cold, a rousing fire
    Upon the social hearth aspire,
And four years old with bountiful design
Bring in the Sabine jar the long-expected wine.
    Leave to th'immortal Gods the rest,
    For when they shall have once supprest
The winds, that on the boiling surge contend,
Nor cypress shakes a leaf, nor yon old ash-trees bend.
    Enquire not of to-morrow's fate,
    And whatsoever chance await,
Turn to account, nor fly from sweet amours,
Nor let the dance be shunn'd by such address as * yours.
    While yet your vig'rous years are green,
    Nor peevish age brings on the spleen,
By turns the field, the tennis-court repeat,
And whispers soft at night for assignations meet.
    Now glad to hear the damsel raise
    The laugh, that her retreat betrays,
Steal from her arm the pledge for theft dispos'd
Or from her finger force, with sham-resistance clos'd.

The pronoun TU being emphatical in the original, it is likely that Thaliarchus was an excellent dancer.

*Whom he praises for his eloquence, his parentage, for the invention of
the lyre and * palestra, for his great address in pilfering, and for the
offices that he discharges.*

O thou, which, eloquent and chaste,
From Atlas sprung, rough man to rule,
And form our sons to toil and taste
    As in th'Athenian school.
Thee will I sing, great Jove's courier,
Inventor of the lyre confest;
Expert to steal and disappear,
    And turn it to a jest.
Thee when a boy, with threats injoin'd
To bring the steers you had withdrawn,
Apollo laugh'd aloud to find
    His quiver also gone.
King Priam likewise, thee his guide,
Deserting Troy with all his wealth,
Atreus his haughty sons defy'd,
    And hostile camp by stealth.
The pious souls to realms of love,
Your golden rod compels to go,
O grateful to the Gods above
    And to the pow'rs below.

*A school for wrestling, and other manly exercises.

He advises Leuconoe to indulge in pleasure, regardless of all care for the morrow, by deducing his arguments from the brevity and fleetness of life.

*Seek not, what we're forbid to know,
    The date the Gods decree
To you, my fair Leuconoe,
    Or what they fix for me.
Nor your Chaldean books consult,
    But chearfully submit,
(How much a better thought it is!)
    To what the Gods think fit.
Whether more winters on our head
    They shall command to low'r,
Or this the very last of all
    Shall bring our final hour.
E'en this, whose rough tempestuous rage
    Makes yon Tyrrhenian roar,
And all his foamy breakers dash
    Upon the rocky shore.
Be wise and broach your mellow wine,
    Which carefully decant,
And your desires proportionate
    To life's compendious grant.
E'en while we speak the moments fly,
    Be greedy of to-day;
Nor trust another for those pranks
    Which we may never play.

In order to imitate the metre of the original, the longest measure in the English tongue (much in use amongst our old poets) is here introduced, but, for convenience of printing, one line is severed into two.

57

Having celebrated the Gods, heroes, and certain famous men, at last
he comes to the divine honours of Augustus.

Clio, to sing on pipe or lyre,
What man, what hero is your choice,
And with what God will you inspire
    Glad echo's mimic voice?
Or in the Heliconian shade,
Or Pindus or cool Hæmus sped,
Where the vague woods at random stray'd
    With Orpheus at their head?
E'en he who, by his mother's art,
The loud cascade, the rapid wind
Cou'd stop—and ears to oaks impart,
    To his soft airs inclin'd?
First then the usual form of praise
Is his, who men and Gods impow'rs,
The earth, the sea, the world he sways,
    The seasons and the hours.
From whom no greater can proceed,
To whom no being's like or near;
Yet Pallas challenges the mead
    Of secondary fear.
Nor thee, brave Liber, will I slight,
Nor thee, fair Forrester, the foe
Of beasts, nor thee which aim'st so right,
    Dread Phœbus, with thy bow.
Alcides next, and Leda's twins,
In chivalry and cestus too
I praise, whose star, when it begins
    To bless the seaman's view,
Its brightness makes the waves subside,
The winds are still, the clouds disperse,
And smooth at their command's the tide,
    That roar'd but now so fierce.
Now shall I Rome's first founder sing,

Or Numa's peaceful reign commend,
Or Priscus great and mighty king,
    Or Cato's glorious end?
Great Regulus I will enroll,
The house of Scaurus, Paulus write,
So lavish of his godlike soul,
    And grateful thee recite,
Fabricius, with rough Curius join'd;
Him and Camillus too for arms
A hardy poverty design'd
    In their paternal farms.
As imperceptibly the pines,
Marcellus, so thy fame aspires:
The Julian star, like Luna, shines
    Amongst the lesser fires.
Sire and preserver of our race,
From Saturn sprung, do thou * convey,
That Cæsar hold the second place
    In thine eternal sway;
Whether o'er Parthia's threatning host
At a just triumph he arrive,
Or, subject to the eastern coast,
    Confed'rate Indians drive.
Subordinate to thee alone,
He o'er the happy world shall reign,
While thou shalt thunder from thy throne
    On each polluted fane.

*A word attempted in the peculiarity of Horace—grant by delegation, make over
your right.

59

He is very uneasy that his rival Telephus is preferred to him by Lydia.

When Lydia to my rival tells
How Telephus, her Telephus excells;
  And harps upon his manly charms,
His neck so rosy-red, and iv'ry arms;
  Alas! I boil with jealous ire,
And all th'internal man is set on fire.
  Then are my pow'rs of reason weak,
My colour comes and goes, and down my cheek
  The trickling tears of anguish steal,
Proof of the ling'ring fever that I feel.
  I burn, if in th'immod'rate broils
Of liquor thy white sleeve the tippler soils,
  Or in a raging am'rous fit,
Has left his mark upon the lips he bit.
  Believe me, Lydia, in the end
You cannot hope his love will long extend,
  Who to your kisses is so rude
By Venus in nectareous balm imbu'd.
  O happy thrice, and thrice again!
Who without breach still hug the pleasing chain;
  Nor ever any bick'ring strife
Can part them till the last extreme of life.

TO THE REPUBLIC OF ROME, ON THE
RENEWAL OF THE CIVIL WAR.

New floods of strife that swell the main,
O ship, shall bring thee out again;
O wherefore venture? 'tis your fort
To keep your station in the port.
Do not you see your sides bereft,
Till not a single oar is left,
And, wounded by the rapid blast,
Groan the crack'd sail-yards and the mast?
Nor are there scarcely farther hopes,
That your old keel, despoil'd of ropes,
Can longer hold it out to brave
The fury of th'impetuous wave.
Thy canvas is no longer tight,
Nor Gods to sue in evil plight,
Tho' once a Pontic pine you stood,
And daughter of a noble wood,
May'st boast a vain descent and form—
The tim'rous seaman in a storm
Trusts not in painted planks—be warn'd,
Lest by the hissing winds you're scorn'd.
Late my vexation and my care,
Still my desire and constant pray'r,
Yet may'st thou from those isles be free
 That glitter in th'Ionian sea.

When Paris ship'd in base deceit,
  Against all hospitable laws,
Fair Helen in th'Idean fleet,
  Nereus injoin'd the winds a pause;
And hush'd into the peace, they hate
  The rapid murm'rers, while he sung
Each cruel circumstance and date
  Of destiny, that o'er them hung.
"Ill-omen'd her you take to Troy,
  "Whom Greece united shall reclaim,
"And Priam's ancient reign destroy,
  "And your connubials with the dame.
"What deaths attend the Dardan realm!
  "What toils for man and steed to bear!
"See Pallas now her shield, her helm,
  "Her car and all her wrath prepare!
"In vain, presumptuous in the aid
  "Of Venus, you your hair shall tire,
"And grateful to each list'ning maid
  "Run soft divisions on the lyre.
"In vain the spears and Cretan dart,
  "So dread to amorous delight,
"You shall avoid with timid heart,
  "And Ajax swift to urge your flight.
"Yet late, too late, adult'rous swain,
  "You shall your locks in dust besmear,
"See there Ulysses, see the bane
  "Of Troy with Pylian Nestor near.
"The Salaminian Teucer speeds—
  "See warlike Sthenelus arrive,
"Who, if there's need of martial steeds,
  "Is excellent those steeds to drive.

"Thou too, Meriones, shall know,
  "And more heroic than his sire
"Hear Diomed, thy deadly foe,
  "In wrath to find thy post inquire.
"Whom you in panting haste shall fly,
  "Tho' Helen heard another tale,
"As harts the wolf they chance to spy,
  "Heedless of pasture in the vale.
"Long as Achilles' wrath shall last,
  "Thy Phrygian dames shall stave their doom,
"But Grecia's flames, some winters past,
  "Shall Trojan tow'rs consume."

He is reduced to sing a recantation; for he begs pardon of a young lady whom he had offended with certain Iambics: and he shifts the blame upon his passionate temper, whose uncontroulable violence he describes.

To that lampoon against your fame,
O fairer than the beauteous dame
That bore thee, put what shameful end you please,
Whether in flaming fire, or Adriatic seas.
Cybele, nor the priest possest,
Phœbus himself an inward guest,
Not Liber can the settl'd temper shake,
Not Corybantian drums with all the noise they make;
Like baleful ire, which neither blade
Of Noric temper has dismay'd;
Nor ship-devouring seas, nor fire-flakes red,
Nor Jove himself up-roaring in tremendous dread.
'Tis said Prometheus was controul'd
To work into the human mould
Some portion took from brutes of every kind,
And to the stomach's pride the lion's wrath assign'd.
'Twas wrath that could Thyestes quell,
By such a downfal, great and fell,
That final overthrow of towns, where now
O'er the raz'd walls the foe drive their insulting plough.
Take warning and suppress your rage;
Me also, in my blooming age,
Such sallies cou'd seduce too far to dare,
And in the keen Iambic satyrize my fair.
But now I would myself endear,
And for the gentle change severe,
Provided she my recantation view,
And be again my sweet, and all my hope renew.

*He invites her to Lucretilis, shewing her sundry advantages that she
should reap from the place.*

   Brisk Faunus oft Lyceus flies,
    And to Lucretilis applies,
  And there defends, in situation sweet,
My goats from showery winds, and from the burning heat.
    Secure without another ward,
    The wives of their unsavoury lord,
  At large on thyme and arbute shrubs are fed,
Nor do their kids fierce wolves or lurking adders dread.
    But more especial is their peace,
    If you the imprison'd notes release,
  And those sweet strains, O Tyndaris, you play,
Ustica's sloping groupe of marble piles repay.
    The Gods protect, the Gods espouse
    My lyric muse, and faithful vows,
  Here you shall fully taste a welcome guest,
The horn of rural honours heap'd for thee and prest.
    Here in a valley's close retreat
    You shall avoid the dog-star's heat,
  And here shall harp upon the Teian string,
Penelope and Circe vying for the king.
    Here shaded, innocent and light,
    You shall partake the Lesbian white,
  Nor to your bow'r shall Mars himself betake,
Nor Semele's Thyoneus his disturbance make.
    And, though suspected to be here,
    You shall not ruffian Cyrus fear,
  Lest his rude hands should not your sex forbear,
But pull your chaplet off, and the poor night-gown tear.

Wine moderately taken, makes the heart glad, but drank to excess, creates madness.

†Varus, you shou'd no tree prefer
   Before the sacred vine,
If you to plant the kindly soil
   Of Catilus design.
For to the droughty all things hard
   Has Heav'n and nature made;
Nor can we rankling care escape
   Without the bottle's aid.
Who make a racket in their cups,
   Of want or war's distress,
Nor rather Bacchus, sire of joy,
   And graceful Venus bless?
But lest we shou'd transgress and take
   More liquor than we ought,
The Centaurean battles warn
   O'er such carousing fought.
Great Bacchus is a warning too
   As most severely just
Against Sithonians right and wrong
   Confounding in their lust.
To thee my candid ‡ Bassareus
   I will not do despite;
Nor bring from underneath the leaf
   What best had shunn'd the light.

Restrain your Berecynthian horn,
    And hush your savage drums,
After whose clam'rous din, self-love
    In partial blindness comes;
Vain glory next, with empty head
    Aloft, is wont to pass;
And tattling treachery succeeds
    Seen through as clear as glass.

*Quintilius Varus having enjoyed great posts, and even the consulship itself at Rome, was at last overthrown in Germany with a very great slaughter, called the Varian defeat, and esteemed most deplorable in the judgment of Augustus. This defeat happened shortly after the death of Horace, which (I suppose) makes Rodellius doubt whether this Quintilius Varus, to whom this ode is addressed, be the same.

† The English metre is the same as in ode the eleventh.

‡ A name of Bacchus, from the Hebrew Bassar, which signifies to work in the vineyard.

That he is inflamed with her love.

The mother of the fierce desires
And Semele the Theban's son inspires,
    And wanton wilfulness assures
To render up my heart to fresh amours.
    Bright Glycera my soul inflames,
Whose lustre e'en the Parian polish shames,
    And her sweet archness fans the blaze,
And slipp'ry looks that balk the lover's gaze.
    Her Cyprus now deserting quite,
Venus on me careers with all her might,
    Nor lets the Scythian be rehears'd,
Nor Parthian furious with his steed revers'd,
    As things impertinent to sing.
Here, lads, in rolls the living verdure bring,
    And frankincense and vervain place
With wine of two years old to crown the vase.
    A victim welt'ring in his gore,
Her presence will propitiate the more.

He invites Mæcenas to an entertainment by no means sumptuous.

Dear knight, with me you shall partake
In sober cups of Sabine wine,
Poor bev'rage of Horatian make,
    Which with these hands of mine
Was well secur'd that very day,
When such applause in thund'ring roar
Was giv'n your merit at the play;
    Till from the sounding shore
Of * your own Tiber, back it came,
And at Mount Vatican arriv'd.
There echo, pleas'd t'augment your fame,
    The gen'ral peal reviv'd.
You on Calenian juice can dine,
And may rich Cæcuban afford;
But Formian or Falernian wine
    Appear not at my board.

Tiber takes its rise from Tuscany, the native country of Mæcenas.

He exhorts the damsels and boys to sing their praises.

Ye tender virgins, Dian sing,
  Ye lads, the smooth fac'd Phœbus praise;
And lov'd so much by heav'n's high king,
  Latona likewise grace the lays.
Praise her that loves the streams and groves,
  Such as cold Algidus o'ershade,
Or in black Erymanthus roves,
  Or Cragus ever verdant glade.
Ye vying youths of Tempe tell,
  And Delos, Phœbus native place;
Him, whom the bow becomes so well,
  And lyre of true Mercurial grace.
He, if he tearful war inflicts,
  Or wretched famine, as you pray,
Against the Persians and the Picts
  From Cæsar shall the plague convey.

Integrity of life is on all sides in security, and that he proves by an instance of himself.

One sound and pure of wicked arts
Leaves to the blacks their spear and bow,
Nor need he deadly tinctur'd darts
    Within his quiver stow.
Whether the suns of southern flame,
Or barb'rous Caucasus he braves,
Or goes, where of romantic fame,
    Vast tracts Hydaspes laves.
For careless, out of bounds to rove,
(A song on Lalage my plan)
Me swordless in the Sabine grove
    A wolf beheld, and ran.
A monster, such as ne'er was fed
In warlike Daunia's beechen plain,
Nor e'er that nurse of lions bred,
    E'en Juba's dry domain.
Me in those lifeless regions place,
Where trees receive no fost'ring gale,
Whence Jove has turn'd away his face,
    And clouds obscure prevail;
Or place me, where the sun too near,
No huts can stand the heat above,
Sweet-smiling, sweetly-prattling dear,
    My Lalage I'll love.

There is no reason why Chloe should shun the touch of man, whom in
the maturity of her bloom she is now fit for.

Me, Chloe, like a fawn you fly,
That seeks in trackless mountains high
    Her tim'rous dam again;
Alarm'd at every thing she hears,
The woods, the winds excite her fears,
    Tho' all those fears are vain.
For if a tree the breeze receives,
That plays upon the quiv'ring leaves
    When spring begins to start;
Or if green lizards, where they hide,
Turn but the budding bush aside,
    She trembles knees and heart.
But I continue my purspit,
Not like the fierce Getulian brute,
    Or tyger, to assail,
And of thee life and limbs bereave—
Think now at last 'tis time to leave
    Thy mother for a male.

Who lamented inconsolably the death of Quintilius.

What can abash the mournful strains,
Or bounds prescribe to grief, like this,
   For those most precious dear remains,
   Of which we have so great a miss?
Melpomene, do thou the dirge inspire,
To whom Jove gave the liquid voice and lyre.

   Has then eternal sleep possess'd
*Quintilius, mod'rate, just and kind,
   Where shall our grievance be redress'd,
   Or where will ye his equal find,
O modesty, and faith, the fair allies
Of justice, and the truth without disguise?

   —— An object of exceeding grief
To many, virtuous, did he fall—
   But thou, O Virgil, art the chief,
   More inconsolable than all—
In vain, alas! you to the Gods resent
Him, who was not on such conditions lent.

   What tho' your own majestic lays
Shou'd, sweeter far than Orpheus' lyre,
· Give ears to laurels and to bays,
   You cou'd not make his corpse respire,
Or bid the blood in that cold image flow,
Which Mercury, the minister below,

   Has to the gloomy crowd compell'd,
In locking up the doors of fate,
   Nor will he be by pray'r withheld,
   However musical and great—
'Tis hard—but manly patience must endure,
And make things lighter, that admit no cure.

This Quintilius is not the same with him to whom the eighteenth ode is addressed, but a native of Cremona, a poet by profession, and a near relation of Virgil; which latter circumstance particularly endeared him to Horace.

He insults her, that now being old, she is deservedly contemned by her gallants.

More sparing the young rakes alarm
The window-shutters of their toast,
You now may sleep secure of harm;
    The door affects the post,
Which mov'd so oft its pliant hinge—
—You hear that serenade no more,
"Sleep'st thou, while dying lovers winge,
    "O Lydia, at thy door!"
Jilt, thou the scoffing sparks shall soon
 Lament, neglected in a lane,
When, at the changing of the moon,
    The north-west blows amain;
While love and vehement desire,
 Such as the mares for stallions seize,
Shall set your blister'd breast afire,
    Join'd to complaints like these,
That gladsome youths on ivy green
 And constant myrtle rather glote;
To Hebrus winter's comrade keen,
    The wither'd leaves devote.

It is not fitting that the votaries of the muses should be liable to solicitude and grief. The poet recommends his friend Lamia to the Pimplean muse.

Friend of the muses, fear and pain
I throw into the Cretan main,
To be the sport of ruffian tempests there—
Who the cold north shall sway is far beyond my care.
I in peculiar unconcern
Profess myself, whatever turn
The great affairs of Tiridates take,
And all th'alarming dread, that keep his thoughts awake.
O muse of the Pimplean hill,
That lov'st to taste the genuine rill,
Weave me those flow'rs that brightest beams receive,
Yea elegance and fragrance for my Lamia weave.
Without that influence of thine,
Vain are the honours I design,
Thou and thy graceful sisters ought to smile,
To him devote new strains, and in the Lesbian style.

This is the same Lamia with him, ode xvii. *book* iii. *where we shall have more occasion to take notice of him.*

That they should not quarrel and fight with their cups, as is the manner of barbarians.

With glasses form'd for joy to fight,
Is what the Thracians do in spite;
Let Bacchus know no bar'brous customs here,
But keep the modest God from bloody discord clear.
Can such strange contraries agree,
As wine and lights in social glee,
And sabres such as savage Media wears—
Cease your vile noise, my friends, nor quit your easy chairs.
Me too!—shall I your revels join,
And sour my good Falernian wine?—
No, let the brother of the Locrian fair,
Rather his lovesick joys, and darling flame declare.
He will not—On no other plan,
No other terms I take my can—
Whatever damsel e'er thy breast inflam'd,
Was of ingenuous birth, nor need you be asham'd.
Whatever be the case speak out
To friendly ears, nor make a doubt.—
"Ah wretch! how thou art hamper'd in a straight,
"A lad, whose matchless worth deserv'd a better fate."
What sorceress, what magic art,
What pow'r divine can ease thy smart?—
E'en Pegasus to clear thee will be loth
From one compos'd of whimsy, * wantonness and wrath.

Chimæra. Προσθε Λnων οπιθεν δε Δρακων, μεσση δε Χιμαιρα.

HOM.

Archytas a philosopher and geometrician is introduced remonstrating
to a certain sailor, that all must die, and beseeching that he would not
suffer his corpse to lie unburied on the shore.

Archytas, born to compass land and sea,
  And of the countless sand thy charts to make,
A little boon of dust suffices thee,
  Which on Matinian shores thy relicks take.
Nor is there profit in those airy dreams,
  When you the houses of the planets try'd,
And the round world determin'd by your schemes,
  Since in your death all these grand projects dy'd.
The sire of Pelops in like manner fell,
  Tho' with the Gods he feasted in the sky;
Tithonus chang'd into a sauterelle,
  And Minos in Jove's secrets wont to pry.
Death too has got * Panthoides again,
  Tho' having taken from the wall his shield,
He cou'd so well the Trojan times explain,
  Nor aught to death but skin and nerves cou'd yield.
This was no mean professor in the ways
  Of truth and nature, as you did presume —
But night, a gen'ral night, its wing displays,
  And all at length must travel to the tomb.
The furies some expose to martial rage,
  The greedy sailors perish in the wave,
The funerals increase of youth and age,
  None from fell Proserpine themselves can save.
Me, e'en Archytas, the outrageous south,
  Upon oblique Orion sure t'attend,
Where that ILLYRIC opes her gulphing mouth,
  Involved at once in an unlook'd-for end.

But thou, O sailor, do not check thy hand,
  Nor grutch on these unburied bones to throw
A little portion of the common sand—
  So may the eastern blasts, whate'er you owe,
Whate'er they threaten to th'Hesperian floods,
  (Thee safe) make Venusinian forrests pay,
And Jove and Neptune, with great store of goods,
  Thee to Tarentum's port, in peace convey.
But shou'd you this benevolence neglect,
  A fraud about to hurt your sons unborn,
Perchance, a due reward you may expect,
  Of equal terror, and of equal scorn.
If not my prayers, my curses must prevail,
  And no atonement can thy conscience clear,
'Tis not so much (tho' you're in haste to sail)
  To sprinkle thrice the dust in kindness here.

*Pythagoras asserted that his identical spirit, about seven hundred years before, was the soul of Euphorbus the son of Panthous, who was slain at the siege of Troy.

See this ode finely imitated by Matthew Prior.

It is a marvel almost up to a prodigy, that Iccius the philosopher, laying aside his studies, should take a turn to arms, through desire of riches.

My friend, you're now invidious grown,
To make th'Arabian wealth your own,
And 'gainst unconquer'd Saba war declare,
And for the bar'brous Mede his future chains prepare.
What virgin, when her love is slain,
Shall be a handmaid in thy train?
And, when thou din'st, what youth from out the court,
Shall stand with essenc'd hair, thy splendour to support?
An archer of paternal craft,
Skill'd to direct the Indian shaft!—
Who now denies but streams their ways may force
Back to the lofty hills, and Tiber change his course,
When you choice books so dearly bought,
On doctrines that Panætius taught,
And your Socratick stock for armour sell,
Whose taste for better things at first set out so well?

He requests the goddess to come to the temple, which Glycera had dedicated to her.

Leave Cyprus, thou that art the queen
   Of Gnidus, and the Paphian isle,
And with my Glycera be seen,
Where, in her temple deck't and clean,
   With frankincense she courts thy smile.

With all his ardour bring thy boy,
   The nymphs, the graces loose and free;
Youth's goddess too, that has no joy,
With Mercury, whose mirth wou'd cloy,
   Without thine influence and thee.

He asks not riches of the God, but only a sound mind in a sound body.

What shall the pious poet pray
Upon the dedication day;
What vow prefer to this Phœbean shrine,
While from the bowl he pours the first-fruits of his wine?
Not the rich crop Sardinia yields,
Nor of Calabria's sunny fields
The herds I ask, nor elephants nor gold,
Nor grounds of which still Liris leaves the tale untold.
Let the Calenian grape be press'd
By those whom fortune has possess'd;
Let the rich merchant in gold cups exhaust
The wine, which to replace his Syrian venture cost:
Dear to the Gods, since thrice or more
In one year he can travel o'er
Th' * Atlantic sea undamag'd, while with me
Sweet olives, mallows light, and succ'ry best agree.
Grant, God of song, this humble lot,
But to enjoy what I have got,
And I beseech thee keep my mind intire
In age without disgust, and with the chearful lyre.

So called from Atlas the highest mountain in Mauritania, which is the extremity of Africa towards the streight of Gades (now Cadiz) beyond which the Romans at that time had but little notion of land.

He addresses his lyre, and requires of it assistance, and that it should not cease to accompany his song.

If e'er at leisure in the shade
  We've play'd a lesson to remain:
My lyre, the like be now essay'd,
  A true Augustan strain.
Thou whom that * Lesbian touch'd so sweet,
  Tho' with his soldiers arms he bore
Val'rous, or moor'd his shatter'd fleet
  Upon the swampy shore.
Yet Venus and her clinging boy,
  And wine to musick wou'd he set,
And on fair maids his skill employ,
  With hair and eyes of jet.
O pride of Phœbus, grateful shell,
  Accepted where the gods regale,
Thou, that can'st sooth my toils so well,
  'Tis Horace bids thee hail!

*Alcæus.

That he should not grieve out of measure, that his rival was unjustly
preferred to him by Glycera.

Tibullus, do not grieve too much,
  Nor in soft elegies complain,
That Glycera's caprice is such,
  And such her insolent disdain,
That she your junior shou'd prefer,
Who looks more amiable to her.

For Cyrus fair Lycoris burns,
  So charming with her little face,
But he the fondling damsel spurns
  For squeamish Pholoe's coy embrace;
But sooner shall the goats be join'd
To wolves of fierce Appulian kind,

Than Pholoe with a filthy rake
  Commit adult'ry, heinous sin,
Such mischief Venus loves to make,
  Who forms and tempers not akin
Pairs with her cruel brazen yoke,
And acts barbarity in joke.

O'er me too in an evil hour
  Had servile Myrtale the sway,
A nymph of more tyrannic pow'r
  Then Adria in Calabria's bay,
Tho' at that time a fairer maid
And gentler did my heart invade.

He repents, that following the Epicureans, he had been wanting in his
zeal to the Gods.

A sparing and unfrequent guest
In Jove's high temple at the best,
While mad philosophy my mind pursu'd,
I now must shift my sail, and have my course renew'd.
For lo! the sempiternal sire
(Who us'd to cleave with brandish'd fire
The clouds, as I conceiv'd) of late was seen,
With car and thund'ring horses in the clear SERENE.
Which the still earth and floods that flow,
And horrid Tænarus below,
And those Atlantic bounds compels to quake;
'Tis God, and God alone pre-eminent can make
The depths emerge, the mighty poor;
'Tis he, that brings to light th'obscure—
And fortune, at his bidding takes a crown,
Here proudly sets it up, there sternly throws it down.

He beseeches her to look to the preservation of Cæsar, then on the
point of going against the Britons.

O Goddess, whose indulgence sways
Fair Antium sounding with thy praise,
Whose influence can exalt the meanest slave,
Or turn triumphant pomps to sorrow and the grave.
  Thee the poor farmer's anxious pray'r
  Solicits, that his fields may bear;
Thee, mistress of the main, the sailor hails,
As his Bithynian bark o'er Cretan billows sails.
  Thee the vague Scythians, Dacian rude,
  And cities, nations unsubdu'd,
The Latian fierce for battle far and near,
Thee the barbaric queens and purple tyrants fear.
  Let not your hurtful foot displace
  The pillar standing on its base,
Nor let the thronging populace rebel,
And roaring out to arms, to arms the state compel.
  *Necessity precedes thy band,
  With nails and wedges in her hand,
Her brazen hand, nor is the hook, nor, hot
With execrable death, the melted lead forgot.
  Thee hope, and faith, so scarce, revere,
  And cloath'd in white are ever near,
And still themselves of your own train profess,
Howe'er you bilk the great, and change your seat and dress.
  The faithless mob and courtezan
  Behave upon another plan;
And all your friends, when they have drank you dry,
The burthen they should share, in base desertion fly.

Yet, yet propitiate Cæsar's scheme
On Britain, and the world's extreme,
And all our new recruits, that well might brave,
The eastern continent, and Erythrean wave.
O fie upon the barb'rous times,
Fraternal wounds, and civil crimes,
What has this iron-age refus'd to do!
What have we left untouch'd, that honest hearts shou'd rue!
Our youth, where have they been restrain'd:
What altars are there left unstain'd—
Yet 'gainst the Scythian and Arabian foe
May all our new-forg'd weapons by thy guidance go!

*Necessity signifies here the last extremity or death, and things mentioned to be-
long to her, were all instruments of torture amongst the Romans.

For whose return from Spain, he rejoices with much exultation.

With the sweet censer and the lyre,
And fatted calf upon the sacred fire,
  The tutelary Gods we bless,
That we our Numida once more caress;
  Who safe and sound from farthest Spain,
Dear to a thousand friends, is come again—
  And yet to none such love he bears,
With none the fond embrace so warmly shares,
  As with lov'd Lamia, mindful still
That they were form'd by one preceptor's skill,
  And both together chang'd their gown—
Set the good day in white memorials down;
  The ready cask by no means spare,
Nor let your feet the morrice-dance forbear.
  Yet Damalis the tippler check,
Lest Bassus she out-drink—the table deck
  With store of parsley, many a rose
And lily, that in transient sweetness blows.
  They all will turn their putrid eyes
On Damalis, who will not quit her prize;
  But her new conquest hugs in hold,
As the ambitious ivies the tall oak infold.

Whom he invites to indulge their geniuses on occasion of the victory at Actium.

To drink and dance with all the glee
Of men that find their country free
Now, now's the time—now deck the hallow'd shrine,
Like Mars his active priests, and make the temple fine.
Before it was no lawful thing
The long-kept Cæcuban to bring,
While for th'imperial capitol the queen
Ruin and wrath prepar'd, and every deadly scene,
With her contaminated train
Of eunuchs, arrogant and vain,
In hopes to compass every point at last,
Drunk with a long success, and her good fortune past.
But now her rage is somewhat tame,
Since scarce a ship escap'd the flame,
And, tho' at large the Egyptian grape she swill'd,
With real horrors now her frantic soul is fill'd.
For as from Italy she flies,
His urgent oar Augustus plies,
And, as the hawk pursues the dove, he rows,
Or sportsman hunts the hare trac'd in Æmonian snows,
That he this monster of her kind
Might in coercive fetters bind—
But she, while for a nobler death she tried,
Nor fear'd the hostile sword, nor sought herself to hide.
Then to her downcast court she went,
With look serene, as in content,
And to her gen'rous veins the aspicks laid,
By pre-determin'd death more fierce and desp'rate made.
For the Liburnian fleet, she grudg'd
The fate to which she was adjudg'd,
A woman of her pow'r and pomp allow'd,
In triumph to be dragg'd before the clam'rous crowd.

He would have him bring nothing for the gracing of his banquet but myrtle.

In the original metre exactly.

Persian pomps, boy, ever I renounce them:
Scoff o'the plaited coronet's refulgence;
Seek not in fruitless vigilance the rose-tree's
    Tardier offspring.
Mere honest myrtle that alone is order'd,
Me the mere myrtle decorates, as also
Thee the prompt waiter to a jolly toper
    Hous'd in an arbour.

*He advises Pollio to forbear the writing of a tragedy for a season, till
the state should be settled. And afterwards he praises his compositions.*

    The war, that rose from civil hate
    In that Metellian consulate,
  Our vices, measures, and the sport of chance,
The famous triple league, the Roman shield and lance,
    With gore unexpiated, smear'd,
    A work whose fate is to be fear'd
  You treat, and on those treacherous ashes tread,
Beneath whose seeming surface glow the embers red.
    O spare a little to repeat
    Your tragic verse severely sweet;
  Soon, when the public weal you shall replace,
Your grand Athenian works again the stage shall grace.
    Thou who defend'st the poor with zeal,
    To whom the conscript house appeal,
  For whom the fertile laurels, that you wore
In that Dalmatian triumph, deathless honour bore.
    E'en now you make my tingling ear
    The din of martial trumpets hear,
  Now clarions bray, and men in armour bright
The routed horse and horsemen with their lightning fright.
    Now mighty captains I perceive,
    In clouds of glorious dust atchieve
  Eternal fame, and all the world their own,
Save the ferocious fire of Cato's soul alone.

Juno and every pow'r propense,
Like her, for Africa's defence,
When unreveng'd they left their darling coast,
Offer'd the victor's grandsons to Jugurtha's ghost,
Say where the blood of Romans slain,
Has not made fertile every plain
Whose monuments record our impious deeds,
And our great downfal heard by the remotest Medes?
What gulphs, what rivers in their flow
Do not our dire dissensions know?
What sea is not discolour'd by the gore
Of Romans basely slain, what climate, or what shore?
But leaving mirth, O do not urge
My Pollio's muse, the Cean dirge—
In some cool grotto sacred to the fair,
With me and sweet Dione touch a lighter air.

He applauds Proculeius for his generosity to his brethren. The contempt of money makes the wise-man and the monarch.

> The hoarded silver is not white,
> Thou foe to metal in the mine,
> Unless by circulation bright
>   And mod'rate use it shine.
> Let * Proculeius live in song,
> A father to his brethren known;
> Fame jealous-wing'd, shall bear along
>   The bounty, he has shown.
> A vaster realm you shall subdue,
> By conq'ring of a greedy mind,
> Than Lybia and the Gades too
>   With either Carthage join'd.
> —The self-indulging dropsy grows,
> Nor slacks its thirst, until the cause
> From out the pallid body flows,
>   And watry pain withdraws.
> The † king restor'd, and repossess'd,
> Not like the crowd fair virtue views,
> Nor numbers him amongst the bless'd,
>   The language to abuse;
> The laurel, diadem and reign
> She more to that great man applies,
> Who looks upon immod'rate gain
>   With unaffected eyes.

*This generous Roman, having several brothers divested of their fortunes, for bearing arms against Cæsar, divided his substance among them.

† Phraates.

93

Either fortune is to be borne with moderation, since the same condition
of mortality equally impends on all.

O Dellius, that art born to die,
On equanimity rely,
As well in adverse days your spirits buoy,
As keep the hour of wealth from light presumptuous joy.
　Whether you lead a life of woes—
　Or in your distant mead repose,
And bless the festal days in rural state,
With right Falernian wine of more interior date,
　Where the tall pine, and the pop'lar white,
　To form a social bow'r delight
With blending boughs, and diligent to glide,
The riv'let urges haste against its winding side.
　To wine and unguents here exhort,
　And roses of a bliss too short,
While circumstance and age allow their leave,
And those black threads of death the fatal sisters weave.
　You must from purchas'd park and seat,
　Which yellow Tiber laves, retreat—
You must retreat, and your appointed heir
Shall soon possess the heaps you pil'd with so much care.
　If rich and of Inachian race,
　Or, poor and from a lineage base,
You daily in th'inclement skies remain,
It matters not, you must remorseless death sustain.
　To one point we are all compell'd—
　The universal urn is held,
From whence, or soon or late, the lot is cast,
And Charon's boat transports the convicts at the last.

There is no reason he should blush for the love he bears to his waiting maid Phyllis, since the same thing has been the case with sundry great men.

O Phoceus, think it no disgrace
 To love your maid, since Thetis heir,
Tho' proud, of old was in your case,
  Briseis was so fair.
—The slave Tecmessa at her feet
 Saw her lord Ajax—Atreus son
Lov'd his fair captive in the heat
  Of conquest, that he won,
When beat by that Thessalian boy,
 The Phrygian host was disarray'd,
And Hector's death, the fall of Troy,
  An easy purchase made.
Who knows what wealth thou hast to claim,
 Rich parents may thy Phyllis grace,
Surely the Gods have been to blame
  To one of royal race.
You cannot think her meanly born,
 Nor worthless cou'd her mother be,
Whose heart has such ingenuous scorn
  For wealth, and love for thee.
Her face, her limbs so form'd t'engage,
 I praise with a safe conscience still—
Shun to suspect a man, whose age
  Is going down the hill.

The most beautiful Lalage is a maiden unripe for a husband, where-
fore the inclination to possess her ought to be restrained.

As yet her tender neck's unbroke,
Nor to confine her in the yoke,
   Will all your skill avail;
As yet she cannot suit her mate,
Nor stand to bear the mighty weight
   Of an impetuous male.
Your little heifer's fancy feeds
On verdant lawns and flow'ry meads,
   Whose haunts she has preferr'd;
And by the streams, which willows shade,
She loves to have her gambols play'd
   With younglings of the herd.
Forbear preposterous desire,
Nor at the eager grape aspire,
   Anon shall autumn speed;
And mark each bunch with blooming blue,
And vary into purple hue
   The clusters ripe to bleed.
She soon shall follow thee of course,
For time goes on without remorse,
   And to her days shall add
The rip'ning years, that make thee old,
And Lalage, maturely bold
   Shall seek a sturdy lad—
Beloved!—coy Pholoe not so well
Nor Chloris celebrated belle,
   With chest erect and white,
As Luna shining o'er the sea,
And smiling with celestial glee,
   Or Cnidian Gyges bright;
Whom if you place amongst the fair
He'll make sagacious strangers stare,
   As puzzl'd in the case;
Nor can they tell his sex with truth,
By reason of his looks and youth,
   And smooth ambiguous face.

He wishes to have Tibur and Tarentum for the retreat of his old age,
whose pleasant situation he extols.

Septimius, who wou'd go with me,
 To Gades, or unconquer'd Spain,
Or Syrtes, where the Moorish sea
    Bids endless tempests reign?
Be Tibur, by a Grecian plann'd,
 A seat for Horace in his years,
Weary alike of sea and land,
    And martial hopes and fears.
From whence if driv'n by cruel fate,
 May I Galesus see in peace,
Where great Phalanthus rul'd in state,
    And watch'd his cover'd fleece.
With me that little angle takes
 Whose honey's of Hymettian zest,
And with the oil Venafrum makes
    Their olives stand the test.
Where Jove gives winter warmth—and length
 To spring,—and Aulon's heights arise,
Rich with those wines, whose luscious strength
    With true Falernian vies.
These scenes to us their site commend—
 Those tow'rs so pleasant to the view:
There the live ashes of thy friend,
    With tears thou shalt bedew.

97

Whose return to his native country he congratulates.

O Pompey! oft reduc'd with me
To danger's last extremity,
When Brutus led the van—what pow'r on high
Restores thy native Gods, and an Italian sky?
Thou principal and dearest friend,
With whom I've made the day suspend
Its course, infringing on the hours of care,
With bays, and precious essence on our shining hair.
With thee I saw * that fatal field,
Where shamefully I left my shield
In rapid flight, when valour's heart was broke,
And threat'ning heroes fell beneath the hostile stroke.
But me Mercurius, much dismay'd,
Quick thro' the midmost foe convey'd
In a thick cloud—Thou wert ingulph'd again
In struggling tides of war upon the swelt'ring plain.
Wherefore to Jove the feast be paid,
And let your weary limbs be laid,
After long warfare, underneath my bay;
Nor spare the casks I destin'd for this joyful day.
Fill the bright tumblers to the brim,
And in oblivious Massic swim,
And from large shells the fragrant unguents pour.
—Who runs to parsley beds, or to the myrtle bow'r,
For cooling crowns? who throws the most
To take the chair and give the toast?
I will the Bacchanalian priests outdo—
'Tis sweet to lose one's wits at this dear interview.

At Philippi.

98

There is no reason to give any credit to Barine, when she swears,
since she grows the handsomer for her perjuries.

If any punishment or curse
 Had made thee thy false oath bewail;
Hadst thou but been one tooth the worse,
    Or lost a single nail;
I shou'd have kept my faith,—but thou
 Shin'st out more tempting and more fair;
And art, by breaking of thy vow,
    Our youth's peculiar care.
'Tis profit, therefore, to deceive
 Thy mother's ashes in a breath,
Stars, moon, and silent heav'n to grieve,
    And Gods, exempt from death.
Yes, Venus laughs, and nymphs, well known
 For mock-simplicity, deride,
And love still whetting on a stone
    His darts in crimson dy'd.
But add to this new dupes abound,
 New slaves, nor will the old relent,
Tho' sworn to quit her impious pound,
    Where their fond hearts are pent.
At thee the jealous mothers pine,
 At thee old churls, and maids new wed,
Lest by that winning air of thine
    Their spouses be misled.

That he would at length desist from bewailing the death of Mystes.

Not show'rs from darkness without end
Upon the shaggy fields descend,
Nor ruffling whirlwinds o'er the Caspian reign
For ever; nor prolong'd month after month remain,
Friend Valgius, on Armenia's heights
Of ice and snow, perpetual freights;
Nor to the North do the plantations groan
Of Garganus, nor ash trees their lost leaves bemoan.
But you, in one continual dirge,
Th'untimely death of Mystes urge,
Nor with the fondness of your grief have done,
When Vesper comes, or flies the bright-careering sun.
Yet * he, who for three ages join'd,
Liv'd an example of mankind,
Did not, for all the remnant of his years,
Antilochus, so loved, lament with ceaseless tears.
No,—nor did Priam and his wife
For Troilus, who lost his life
In ruddy youth, with endless grief deplore,
And ev'n his tender sisters in a while forbore.
Cease from the softness of your grief,
And let us rather sing our chief,
The great Augustus has new trophies won,
And bade the stiff Niphates with submission run.
Euphrates too must roll his tide
In billows more remote from pride,
And those Gelonians, added to our reign,
Must in the bounds prescrib'd their cavalry restrain.

*Nestor.

A mean is to be observed in either fortune.

A better plan of life you form,
 Not wholly launching out from land,
Nor over-jealous of a storm,
    Too much for shore to stand.
Whoever loves the golden mean,
 From sordid want himself supports,
Nor safe and sober is he seen
    In envy-moving courts.
Tall pines are shaken, and the tow'r
 Comes heaviest from the highest wall,
And thunderbolts, with greater pow'r,
    On topmost mountains fall.
Hearts, well prepar'd, will see a dawn
 Of hope in woe—in wealth will pray
'Gainst change—heav'n brings the winter on,
    And drives the hag away.
If times are evil, by and by
 They shall be better—Phœbus plays
At times upon his minstrelsy,
    Not always shoots his rays.
When times are hardest, then a face
 Of constancy and spirit wear;
But wise contract your sails apace,
    When once the wind's too fair.

That waiving cares we should live merrily.

Whate'er the warlike Spaniard tries,
Or what the Scythian bands devise,
By Adria's sea disjoin'd, cease to enquire,
Nor bustle for a life, whose term should check desire.
　　Smooth youth and beauty must give way
　　To wrinkles dry, and ringlets grey,
Which from gallants their wanton loves divorce,
And drive away sweet slumbers from their eyes of course.
　　Not always does the vernal pride
　　Of flow'rs remain, nor moon abide
In one gay face—Your thoughts why do you teize,
Not made for disquisitions so sublime as these?
　　Why do we not secure our seat
　　Beneath this plane-tree from the heat;
Or thrown at random underneath this pine,
Drink, while we may presume, and essenc'd roses twine
　　In wreathes about our hoary hair,
　　For Bacchus drives off biting care.
Who's there? This same Falernian is too strong,
The passing brook shall quench it, as it purls along.
　　Who shall decoy that gadding lass,
　　Lyde, to come and take a glass?
Bid her with iv'ry lyre mature her haste,
And hair ty'd up behind in the true Spartan taste.

Weighty and tragical subjects are not proper for the Lyric stile.
Horace will sing of nothing but the beauty of Lycymnia, and matters
pertaining to love.

Numantia's fierce and bloody wars,
And Hannibal, your taste abhors,
    Too dire a subject for a song;
Nor staining the Sicilian sea,
Can Carthaginian blood to me
    And to my warbling lyre belong.
Nor can the Lapithan malign,
Nor over-charg'd with heady wine,
    Hyleus suit the lyric strain,
Nor any giant son of earth,
The victim of Herculean worth,
    And dread of Saturn's golden reign.
But, O Mæcenas, as for you,
You will for great Augustus do
    Far better in historic prose:
With more address you'll tell than sing
The story of full many a king,
    That drag'd in pomp triumphal goes.
Me the harmonious muse allures,
To chant my lady fair, and yours,
    And praise Lycymnia's charming voice,
And eyes, that sparkle like the spheres,
With faithful heart, that never veers,
    When she's once settled in her choice.

She's graceful in each bright advance,
Whether she lead the seemly dance,
  Or urge the brilliant repartees,
Or with the noble damsels play,
That honour Dian's holiday,
  Uniting dignity and ease.
Would you in earnest change one lock
Of sweet Lycymnia, for the stock
  That rich Achemenes possess'd,
Or fertile Phrygia's wealthy fleece,
Or all Arabia's ambergreese,
  And houses with all plenty bless'd.
While she declines her blooming cheek,
Where you the burning kisses seek,
  With such benevolent disdain,
And what she'd rather have, than thee,
Refuses, till she makes so free
  As to devour them all again.

Book II.   UPON THE TREE BY WHOSE SUDDEN FALL Ode XIII.
            HE HAD LIKE TO HAVE BEEN CRUSHED.

It is never sufficiently evident what a man ought to beware of——the
praises of Sappho and Alceus.

'Twas on a luckless day, O tree,
 Whatever hand transplanted thee,
And impious bade thee prosper to disgrace
The village of his birth, and crush his future race.
 He could, no doubt, to death devote
 His sire, or cut his mother's throat,
Or sprinkle his unhospitable ground
At night with stranger's blood, or Colchian drugs compound.
 Or whatsoe'er we may conceive
 Of desp'rate feats he could atchieve,
O log, the man that plac'd thee in my farm,
Hurl'd on thy master's head, that did not dream of harm.
 We never are enough aware
 What we should seek, or what forbear—
From Bosphorus the sailor dreads his fate,
Nor heeds what doom at Carthage may his days await.
 The soldiers fear the pointed reed,
 And Parthian shooting in full speed,
The Parthian fears the Roman strength and chain,
One common lot for all remains, and will remain.

How near but now the lot was mine,
So see the gloomy Proserpine,
And Eäcus his dread judicial seat,
And those Elysian fields, where melancholy sweet
  Sappho the sland'rous maids of Greece
  Arraigns, and in a fuller piece
Alceus sings, upon his golden lyre
The conquest or the flight by sea and land how dire!
  Each of these hands th'admiring ghost
  In holy silence hears, but most
Th'attention and the thicking throng augment,
To hear of patriot fights, and kings in exile sent.
  What wonder! since such strains as these
  The many-headed beast can please,
Who hangs his hellish ears, and furies list,
While from their wreathed locks delighted snakes untwist.
  Nay more, Prometheus, and the sire
  Of Pelops to the sound respire,
Nor 'gainst the ounce or lions of the chace,
Will now Orion urge his visionary race.

Life is short, and death inevitable.

Ah! Posthumus, the years, the years
Glide swiftly on, nor can our tears
Or piety the wrinkl'd age forfend,
Or for one hour retard th'inevitable end.
   'Twould be in vain, tho' you should slay,
   My friend, three hundred beeves a day
To cruel Pluto, whose dire waters roll,
Geryon's threefold bulk, and Tityus to controul.
   This is a voyage we all must make,
   Whoe'er the fruits of earth partake,
Whether we sit upon a royal throne,
Or live, like cottage hinds, unwealthy and unknown.
   The wounds of war we scape in vain,
   And the hoarse breakers of the main;
In vain with so much caution we provide
Against the southern winds upon th'autumnal tide.
   The black Cocytus, that delays
   His waters in a languid maze,
We must behold, and all those Danaids fell,
And Sysiphus condemn'd to fruitless toil in hell.
   Lands, house, and pleasing wife, by thee
   Must be relinquish'd; nor a tree
Of all your nurseries shall in the end,
Except the baleful cypress, their brief lord attend.
   Thy worthier heir the wine shall seize
   You hoarded with a hundred keys,
And with libations the proud pavement dye,
And feasts of priests themselves shall equal and outvie.

So great our palaces are now,
They'll leave few acres for the plough.
Wide as the Lucrine lake canals extend,
And sterile planes in sum the wedded elms transcend.
Then violet beds, and myrtle bow'rs,
And all the nosegay-blending flow'rs,
Shall far and wide their spicy breath renew,
Where for their former lords the fertile olives grew.
There the thick laurel's green array
Shall ward the fervid beams of day.
Not so our founder's will, or Cato's lore,
And all our bearded sires commanded things of yore.
Their private fortunes were but small,
But great the common fund of all.
No grand piazzas did there then remain
To catch the summer breezes of the northern wain.
Nor did they, by their edicts wise,
The providential turf despise,
Those laws, which bade each public pile be grand,
And with new stone repair'd, the holy temples stand.

All men covet peace of mind, which cannot be acquired either by
riches or honours, but only by restraining the appetites.

When o'er the Ægean vast he sails
  The seaman sues the gods for ease,
Soon as the moon the tempest veils,
    Nor sparkling guide he sees.
Ease by fierce Thracians in the end;
  Ease by the quiver'd Mede is sought;
By gems, nor purple bales, my friend,
    Nor bullion to be bought.
Not wealth or state, a consul's share,
  Can give the troubled mind its rest,
Or fray the winged fiends of care,
    That pompous roofs infest.
Well lives he, on whose little board
  Th'old silver salt-cellar appears,
Left by his sires—no sordid hoard
    Disturb his sleep with fears.
Why with such strength of thought devise,
  And aim at sublunary pelf,
Seek foreign realms? Can he, who flies
    His country, 'scape himself?
Ill-natured care will board the fleet,
  Nor leave the squadron'd troops behind,
Swifter than harts, or irksome sleet
    Driv'n by the eastern wind.

If good, the present hour be mirth;
 If bitter, let your smiles be sweet,
Look not too forward—nought on earth
    Is in all points complete.
A sudden death Achilles seiz'd,
 A tedious age Tithonus wore—
If you're amerc'd, fate may be pleas'd
    To give to me the more.
A hundred flocks around thee stray,
 About thee low Sicilian kine,
And mares apt for thy carriage neigh,
    And purple robes are thine.
Me, born for verse and rural peace,
 A faithful prophetess foretold,
And groundlings, spirited from Greece,
    In high contempt I hold.

If he was to die, Horace has no inclination to survive him.

Why do you send to break my heart
With your complaints? We must not part;
Nor can th'immortal gods consent, nor I,
My glory and my guard, that thou the first shouldst die.
　　Ah! if a more untimely fate
　　On thee, my soul's ally, should wait,
Why should I keep the wretched remnant here,
Imperfect without thee, and never half so dear?
　　One day shall be the last of both;
　　I have not made a traitor's oath—
Yes, we will go, together will we go,
If you precede, I follow to the shades below.
　　Me nor Chimera breathing fire,
　　Nor Gyas, if he could respire,
With all his hundred hands, should force from thee;
So justice, heav'nly pow'r, and so the fates decree,
　　If Libra rul'd my natal hour,
　　Or Scorpio's more unlucky pow'r,
Ey'd with the menace of an early grave,
Or Capricorn, the tyrant of the western wave.
　　Our horoscope, at all events,
　　Ev'n to a miracle consents—
Thee, lucid Jove, sav'd from Saturnian spite,
And clipt the wings of fate, and stopt its rapid flight,
　　Upon the day the crouded town
　　Thrice hail'd in claps thy just renown—
Me near that time a falling trunk had brain'd,
If Faunus, shield of bards, had not the stroke refrain'd.
　　These mercies therefore bear in mind,
　　And bring the victims you design'd,
And build the fane you vow'd upon the spot;
A slaughter'd lamb from me will suit my humbler lot.

111

He asserts himself to be contented with a little fortune, where others
labour for wealth, and the gratification of their desires, as if they were
to live for ever.

Gold or iv'ry's not intended
 For this little house of mine,
Nor Hymettian arches, bended
 On rich Afric pillars, shine.
For a court I've no ambition,
 As not Attalus his heir,
Nor make damsels of condition
 Spin me purple for my wear.
But for truth and wit respected,
 I possess a copious vein,
So that rich men have affected
 To be number'd of my train.
With my Sabine field contented,
 Fortune shall be dunn'd no more;
Nor my gen'rous friend tormented
 To augment my little store.
One day by the next's abolish'd,
 Moons increase but to decay;
You place marbles to be polish'd
 Ev'n upon your dying day.
Death unheeding, though infirmer,
 On the sea your buildings rise,
While the Baian billows murmur,
 That the land will not suffice.

What tho' more and more incroaching,
 On new boundaries you press,
And in avarice approaching,
 Your poor neighbours dispossess;
The griev'd hind his gods displaces,
 In his bosom to convey,
And with dirty ruddy faces
 Boys and wife are driven away.
Yet no palace grand and spacious
 Does more sure its lord receive,
Than the seat of death rapacious,
 Whence the rich have no reprieve.
Earth alike to all is equal,
 Whither would your views extend?
Kings and peasants in the sequel
 To the destin'd grave descend.
There, tho' brib'd, the guard infernal
 Would not shrewd Prometheus free;
There are held in chains eternal
 Tantalus, and such as he.
There the poor have consolation
 For their hard laborious lot;
Death attends each rank and station,
 Whether he is call'd or not.

Filled with the deity, the poet sings his praises.

Bacchus I saw the other day
  (Posterity believe my lay)
Teaching the science of poetic feet,
While nymphs and satyrs listen'd in the rocks secrete.
  Ha! ha! this lab'ring breast of mine
  Is shock'd anew—and fraught with wine;
My heart is joy—ha! ha! my Bacchus spare,
Nor rear thine ivy wand too terrible to bear.
  Now the mad Thyads I can sing,
  Which struck out wine's perennial spring;
And rivers that with milky current glide,
And honey trickling down from hollow rocks beside.
  Now can I sing the brilliant dame
  Of heav'n, thy celebrated flame,
The tow'rs of Pentheus levell'd with the ground,
And downfal of Lycurgus to thy praise resound.
  You turn the rivers to the main,
  You those barbarian seas restrain,
You in the sacred mountains debonaire
Bind in serpentine knot unhurt your handmaid's hair.
  You, when the bands of giants rose
  Th'almighty father to depose,
The lion's fangs and horrid jaws assum'd,
Drove Rhœcus back to earth, and to destruction doom'd.
  Tho' dance, and lively jests, and sport
  For thee were fitter by report,
Nor did your military talents strike,
Yet facts have shewn thee proof for peace and war alike.
  Thee with your golden horn bedight,
  Saw Cerberus devoid of spite,
And when from hell you made your last retreat,
His tail he kindly wagg'd, and gently lick'd your feet.

*Horace supposing himself changed into a swan, will fly all the world
over; from which adventure he infers, that his poetry will be immortal.*

    Above the vulgar and the trite
    Transform'd, the poet takes his flight
  Thro' heav'n, and will be held on earth no more;
But o'er th'abodes of man, of envious man, shall soar.
    Not I, the poor man's offspring scorn'd;
    Not I thus honour'd and adorn'd,
  As by Mæcenas to be call'd his friend,
Shall know the Stygian stream, or share a common end.
    Now, ev'n but now, my skin began
    To roughen, and my upper man
Of a white bird the radiant form assumes,
And on my hands and neck spring forth the glossy plumes.
    Now a melodious swan indeed,
    Th'Icarian flight I shall exceed;
  And Bosphorus his roaring rocks will know,
And Syrtes, and the plains of Hyperborean snow.
    The Dacians who so poorly feign
    To hold the Romans in disdain;
  The Colchan and Gelonians far remote,
And skilful Spain and Gaul shall learn my works by rote.
    No dirges, squalid grief, or moan,
    At mine unreal death be shown;
  Your loud lamentings at my grave restrain,
Nor care to build the tomb this verse has render'd vain.

A happy life is effected not by wealth and honours, but by peace of mind.

I hate the mob, and drive them hence,
Lost to all sanctity and sense;
Hist to the Muse's priest! hist I implore—
I sing for maids and youths the strains unheard before.
Dread sovereigns their own people sway,
But Jove the kings themselves obey;
He which in triumph hurl'd the giants down,
And rules the universe by his commanding frown.
One man, perhaps, out-plants his friend,
In rows that regular extend;
Another comes more noble to the poll,
Another pleads his fame, and uncorrupted soul;
Another will th'ascendant claim
For clients—but 'tis all the same;
Necessity demands us, dross and scum,
And shakes the labell'd lots, and out they all must come.
He, o'er whose head the naked steel
Impends, will make no hearty meal
From rich Sicilian fare—his sleep no more
The chirping of the birds or harpers will restore—
Sweet sleep's the lusty lab'rer's lot:
Sleep does not scorn the lowly cot,
Nor trees that o'er the riv'let interweave,
Nor Tempe, where the zephyrs play their pranks at eve.
He who desires but neighbour's fare,
Will for no storm or tempest care;
Him setting bear nor rising goat offends,
Nor all the wizzard wit of diarist portends.

Not vineyards beaten by the hail;
  Not flattering farm, whose symptoms fail,
The trees now laying blame upon the showers,
Now winter's pinching hand, or hot sidereal pow'rs.
  The fishes feel the waters shrink,
  Such loads into the depths they sink;
Here many a proud surveyor with his slaves,
And owner of the land, incroach upon the waves.
  But fear and conscience with her cries
  Aboard with the possessor flies;
Nor care will from the top-mast head recede,
And, when he lands, she mounts behind him on his steed.
  What if nor stone in Phrygia hewn
  Can keep the troubl'd mind in tune,
Nor purple brighter than the painted sky,
Nor rich Falernian grape, nor Persian luxury;
  Why should I set about a pile,
  High-pillar'd in the modern stile—
A bait for envy?—Why should I exchange
For cumbersome expence my little Sabine grange?

Lads must be habituated from their tender years to poverty, warfare,
and a laborious life.

Train'd up, my friends, in toil severe,
Let the young lad no hardship fear;
But learn against fierce Parthians to advance,
And on the gallant steed shake his tremendous lance.
And let him lead a life of care
In bustle and the open air—
Him from the wall the tyrant's consort spies,
And marriageable virgin sends her broken sighs.
"Ah me! for fear my royal spouse
"Should this ungovern'd lion rouze,
"And with inferior skill provoke his rage,
"Which breaks thro' thickest ranks the midmost war to wage."
'Tis sweet, 'tis seemly ev'n to die
For one's dear country—should'st thou fly,
Death will pursue the youth afraid to fight,
Nor spares his timid knees, and back, when turn'd to flight.
Virtue which in the spirit tow'rs,
And cannot, like this clay of ours,
Sustain repulse, her fame unsully'd sees,
Nor takes, nor quits her office, as light voters please.
Virtue, to those that may not die,
Opes the strait doors of heav'n on high,
And with her wings in stretch for that sublime,
Scorns the unletter'd mob, and sordid earth, and time.
There's likewise an undoubted meed
For silence, that its faith can plead;
Him that mysterious rites has blaz'd—with me,
Nor tent, nor tilt shall cover, or by land or sea.
Oft the great regent of the day,
If thoughtless man neglect to pray,
In the same lot have vice and virtue cast,
Justice, tho' lame and blind, will take her due at last.

Book III.   ODE III.

A man of virtue is in dread of nothing. The speech of Juno concerning the destruction of Troy, of the end of the Trojan war, and of the Roman empire, which was to take its rise from the remnant of the Trojans.

A man of truth and honour prov'd,
  And in his great resolves unmov'd,
No clam'rous mob his principles can stir,
Nor ev'n a tyrant's threat his manly heart deter.
  No—nor the south, whose dread command
  Fierce Adria's waves cannot withstand,
Nor thund'ring Jove—the universe might fall,
And not disturb his thoughts, or make him shrink at all.
  It was upon no other plan
  That Pollux was so great a man,
And wand'ring Hercules atchiev'd the skies—
Augustus too with them to rites divine shall rise.
  'Twas by no other art than this,
  O Bacchus, sire of social bliss,
Thine unbroke tygers drew thee to the stars,
And Romulus 'scap'd death upon the steeds of Mars.
  For to the Gods in council join'd
  Juno thus spake her gracious mind—
"A foreign whore, and that dire * umpire's lust,
"Has Troy, ev'n Troy reduc'd to downfal and the dust.
  "By me and chaste Minerva doom'd,
  "E'er since Laomedon presum'd
"The gods to rob of their most due reward,
"And subjects shar'd the fate of their deceitful lord.
  "No more that ignominious guest
  "Is of the Spartan dame possest,
"Nor Priam's perjur'd house prevails to break,
"By Hector's strength alone, the forces of the Greek.

"War by our diff'rent int'rests drawn
"To such a length, is past and gone—
"Henceforward I my wrath to Mars give o'er,
"And hatred for the son the Trojan priestess bore.
"Him will I suffer and befriend
"Heav'n's lucid mansions to ascend,
"To take his fill from our nectareous bowl,
"And in the rank of gods his titles to enroll—
"On this condition, that there be
"'Twixt Troy and Rome a raging sea
"For many a league—and let their exiles reign
"And prosper where they will—so that there still remain
"O'er Paris and o'er Priam's clay
"The trampling herd, the beast of prey,
"And cubs secure—The Capitol shall tow'r,
"And vanquish'd Medes confess proud Rome's imperial pow'r.
"Let her extend her fame and fear
"To every region far and near,
"Where the mid-sea from Europe Afric rives,
"And where o'erflowing Nile the fertile land revives.
"Deriving from contempt of gold
"A spirit great and uncontroul'd—
"Gold best unsought, and cover'd in the sand,
"Rather than coin'd for use with sacrilegious hand.
"Whatever pole or place be found
"To give the world his utmost bound,
"There let them pride their armies to engage,
"Both where cold mists descend, or torrid sun-beams rage.

"But this their fate my word confirms
"For Romans on these only terms—
"That they should not an ill-judg'd zeal embrace,
"Nor think their mother-town they prosper to replace.
"If Troy's estate should grow again,
"Again their thousands must be slain,
"Whilst I, Jove's sister and his wife, command
"Against their rising works a new victorious band.
"If thrice their walls of brass should rise,
"By Phœbus helping from the skies,
"Thrice should my Grecian champions lay it low;
"Thrice leave their dames and sons to widowhood and woe."
But whither, Muse, do you aspire?
These subjects are not for the lyre—
Too grand and grave—cease, wanton, to rehearse
The converse of the gods in light degrading verse.

*Alluding to the judgment of Paris.

Book III.   ODE IV.

The poet mentions his being delivered by the assistance of the Muses from sundry perils, and that it has turned out bad for all that have attempted to act against the gods.

Descend from yonder bright serene,
And sing, Calliope, my queen,
A longer strain—or with your warbling tongue,
Or, if you choose, the lute, or lyre by Phœbus strung.
    Hear ye not plain? Or is my thought
    By a transporting frenzy wrought?
I seem to hear sweet sounds, and seem to rove
Where pleasant airs and streams pass thro' th'Elysian grove.
    Me tir'd to sleep, and yet a child,
    From kind Apulia's bounds beguil'd,
Up in mount Vultur, now so fam'd and known,
The woodland doves conceal'd with foliage newly blown;
    Which was a miracle to tell
    By all th'inhabitants that dwell
High-nested on the Acherontian brow,
Or Bantine chace possess, or fat Ferentum plow.
    That I should there securely sleep,
    Nor bears should rush, nor vipers creep;
That sacred bays and myrtle should combine
To hide the dauntless boy by providence divine.
    Yours, O ye Muses! yours intire,
    I to the Sabine heights aspire—
Me, whether cool Preneste shall invite,
Or Tibur sweetly slop'd, or Baian baths delight.
    Me, fond of all your sylvan scene
    Your founts and gambols on the green;
Not all our hopes Philippi render'd void,
Nor rough Sicilian wave, nor cursed tree destroy'd.
    Whenever you shall be with me,
    Chearful I'll sail upon the sea
Of raging Bosphorus, or go by land
Through all the length and drougth of that Assyrian sand.

Th'unhospitable Picts, the race
Of quiver'd Scythia, will I face;
And Concanum, with blood of horses fed,
And Tanais, secure from detriment and dread.
You Cæsar, of such high renown,
Soon as he quarters in each town
His wearied legions, bid his labours cease,
And in Pierian grottoes multiply his peace.
You kindly mod'rate measures urge,
Rejoicing to refrain the scourge—
We know him who alone the Titans quell'd,
And hurl'd in thunder down the monsters that rebell'd—
Ev'n he that rules the stormy main,
The sluggish earth, and Pluto's reign,
And all above, and all beneath the sun,
Both gods and men commands, omnipotent and one.
Depending upon strength of arm,
Those desp'rate youths with dire alarm
Insulted Jove, while all the brethren vie
With Pelion on Olympus to ascend the sky.
But Rhœcus and strong Mimas too,
Or what could huge Porphyrion do,
Or what Typhœus, or with trees up-torn
Enceladus assaulting heav'n in impious scorn,
Rushing against the sounding targe
Of Pallas?—Here a furious charge
Was made by Vulcan—there heav'n's royal dame,
And he, who never quits his golden quiver, came,
Who in the pure Castalian spring
Laves his loose locks, who is the king
Of Lycian wilds, Apollo is his name,
Who Patara and Delos holds by natal claim.

Force void of counsel rushes down
  By its own weight—but there's a crown
Of blest event for courage mixt with care;
But rashness heav'n detests, as working for despair.
  That Gyas with his hundred hands,
  Whose story upon record stands,
 And he * th'attempter of the spotless maid,
Slain by Diana's dart, confirm what we have said.
  The earth her groaning bosom heaves,
  And for each bury'd monster grieves,
 To dismal hell by thund'ring vengeance doom'd.
Nor by the eager flames is Ætna yet consum'd.
  The bird that on the liver preys
  Of Tityus, ever-vengeful stays—
 Three hundred chains Perithous confine,
And gall his am'rous flames, which burn'd for Proserpine.

*Orion.

The applause of Augustus, the dispraise of Crassus, the constancy of Regulus, and his return to the Carthaginians.

The thund'rer, as in heav'n supreme,
We from his dreadful bolts esteem;
And Cæsar, like a god, directs our helm,
Picts and vexatious Persians added to our realm.
Have they, who under Crassus fought,
With base barbarian wives been caught,
And (O inverted manners, alter'd times!)
With step-fathers grown old in foreign slavish climes?
The Marsian and Appulian band,
Beneath an haughty Mede's command,
Forgetting * Numa's shields, and name, and gown,
Jove's Capitol, and Rome subsisting in renown!
The soul of Regulus the great
Precluded such a shameful fate,
Scorning all base conditions ev'n in thought,
As exemplary bad, with future mischief fraught:
If not unpity'd and unspar'd,
Their doom the captive youth had shar'd—
"I've seen seen our standard hung up for a show,
"And troops by Punic foes disarm'd without a blow.
"I've seen our citizens confin'd,
"Ty'd with their free-born arms behind;
"The hostile gates op'd in defiance wide,
"And fields we ravag'd, till'd in ostentatious pride.
"What! shall the soldier bought and sold
"Be braver when exchang'd for gold?
"You add but loss unto an impious stain,
"The poison'd wool its whiteness never can regain,
"Nor valour, wrought to a reverse,
"Can be repair'd by worse and worse—
"If rescu'd from the toils, the tim'rous deer
"Will turn and fight the hounds—then he shall cease to fear,
"Who once has trusted to deceit;
"And shall the Punic host defeat
"Another time—who felt a ruffian tie
"His coward hands with thongs, and was asham'd to die.

"Such, helpless where to fix a ground
"For hope, could peace and war confound—
"O shame! O Carthage! infamously great
"By our confirm'd disgrace, and Rome's subverted state!"
   'Tis said, from his chaste wife's embrace,
   And little boys, he turn'd his face,
And look'd as one amerc'd upon the dust,
With aspect manly stern, determin'd to be just,
   Until the conscript fathers all,
   With council most original,
 He did confirm—and 'midst his friends' dismay
And tears, the godlike exile forc'd himself away.
   And yet full clearly did he know
   The torments he should undergo—
 But waving all his kin with unconcern,
And crowds of Roman people grutching his return,
   He cooly took his leave, as one,
   The business of the forum done,
 Goes for vacation to Venafran lands,
Or where Tarentum, built by † that fam'd Spartan, stands.

Numa's shields—oval bucklers, used by the priests in processions, one of which being sent down from heaven, was esteemed a token of the establishment of the empire; which, that it might not be known or stolen away, Numa commanded eleven more to be made exactly like it, and to be kept in the temple of Mars.

† Phalantus.

Ye Romans, tho' not done by you,
Ye must your fathers' vices rue,
Unless the holy temples ye repair,
And images defil'd with filth and blackness there.
You justly claim imperial sway,
As ye th'immortal gods obey;
Thence your beginning, there refer th'event;
Oft heav'n, for our neglect, has doleful vengeance sent.
Now twice Moneses and the band
Of Pacorus has made a stand
Against our luckless troops, and glad in scorn
Equestrian collars seiz'd, their trinkets to adorn.
While discord is our business grown,
Almost we have been overthrown
By Moors and Dacians, those by sea so dread,
And these expert for jav'lins whirling at our head.
Fraught with offence, at first the times
Defil'd us with domestic crimes,
Our marriage-beds, and families, and race,
Whence all these murders sprang, and national disgrace.
Our virgins, now no longer shy,
Are proud th'Ionic step to try,
And move by leud prescription in their bloom,
And meditate on incest from the mother's womb.
Soon, when her husband's at his wine,
To younger sinners she'll incline,
Nor care with whom the lawless bliss she prove,
In hasty stealth, when once the candles they remove.

128

But, not without her consort's leave,
  She boldly rises to receive
Some broker, that will buy her to his arms,
Or Spanish dupe, that pays full dearly for her charms.
  'Twas not a race from sires like these
  That stain'd with Punic blood the seas,
Slew Pyrrhus and Antiochus the Great,
And beat Hamilcar's son at such a glorious rate;
  But a rough set of manly blades,
  And skillful with the Sabine spades
To turn the glebe, and carry clubs of oak
Such as their rigid mothers from the wood bespoke.
  What hour the sun the shades enlarg'd,
  And from the yoke the steers discharg'd,
Fatigu'd with toil, and urg'd with rapid flight
The time for friendly sleep, or neighbourly delight.
  What does not mould'ring time impair!
  Worse than their sires our fathers were,
And we, far worse than them, about to fill
The world with baser men, and more degen'rate still.

He consoles her in her sorrow for her absent husband, and admonishes her to preserve the faith she had plighted to him.

Asterie, why do you bewail
  Him, whom the zephyrs shall restore,
Which fill with vernal breath the sail,
  Wafting Bithynian wealth on shore,
The happy Gyges, whose fair truth is known,
And constancy has made so much your own?
  He, driv'n by that autumnal * goat
  And southern winds, is forc'd away,
  His meditations to devote
  On fair Asterie night and day,
And joyless, sleepless, spends the year,
With many a melancholy tear.
  And yet the busy footman speeds
  And many a subtle art he tries,
  To urge how Chloe burns and bleeds,
  And how she pines, and how she dies:
And, anxious to receive him to her bed,
Has many such like stories in her head,
  "How a false woman could persuade
  "King Prœtus, credulous too much,
  "With false pretences that she made
  "To murder him, who shunn'd the touch
"Of all impurity and shame,
"The chaste Bellerophon by name.

130

"How Peleus was condemn'd almost
"To hell, in that he had abstain'd,
"And wary 'scap'd the am'rous post
"Where fair Hippolyte remain'd."
And mentions many a novel tale,
That teaches mortals to be frail.
  In vain—for deafer than the rocks
  Of Icarus he hears the lure,
  And as temptation's voice he mocks,
  Asterie, thou art still secure—
And yet—Enipeus—give me leave—
Do not with so much joy receive.
  Tho' (to be fair) no man can ride
  Upon the Martian plain so well:
  A goodly sight, of gallant pride,
  And skill equestrian to excel;
Nor any active man alike
Can through the yielding Tibur strike.
  Soon as the day begins to close,
  Shut up the doors, shut up the gate,
  Nor in the street yourself expose,
  Nor for the scurvy minstrels wait—
The more they call you hard and hard,
The more your doors and ears be barr'd.

*When the constellation of the goat sets at the close of autumn, it generally stirs up
showers and storms.

Maecenas is not to wonder why Horace celebrates the calends of March, notwithstanding he has no wife.

Why, on the * first of March, so clean,
　Free from the matrimonial god,
Why flow'rs and frankincense are seen,
And what these heaps of fewel mean
　　Upon the living sod,
Friend, is from your discernment hid,
　Tho' Greek and Latin are your own.
Know then I vow'd a feast and kid
To † him, who did my death forbid,
　When down the tree was blown.
This day, the chief of all by far,
　A special festival denotes,
And shall remove from out the jar
The cork smok'd down with pitch and tar,
　When Tullus had the votes.
Take, for the safety of thy friend,
　An hundred bumpers at the least;
On high the wakeful lamps suspend,
Let wrath and clamour have an end,
　Nor interrupt our feasts.
Cease each political conceit,
　Nor Rome let all your cares engage;
The Dacian Cotison is beat,
The hostile Medes, in self-defeat,
　Domestic warfare wage:
The Spanish foe now pays the tax,
　Though by slow steps this wreath was won;
The Scythian troops their bows relax,
And, fearful of the Roman ax,
　The field of battle shun:
The state, not as a man in pow'r,
　But as a private friend, repute;
Leave things that are severe and sour
For pleasures of the present hour,
　Wine, converse, harp, and lute.

The calends of March were sacred to Juno, and particularly celebrated by married men and their wives.

† *Bacchus.*

It is a Dialogue concerning their former loves, with a proposal for renewing them.

HO. Whilst my growing flame you nourish'd,
  Spotless of a rival's touch,
 Clasp'd within your arms I flourish'd,
  Not the Persian king so much.
LY. Ere you languish'd for another,
  And with Chloe was inflam'd,
 Lydia, greater than the mother
  Of the Roman race, was nam'd.
HO. Me indeed that Thracian beauty,
  Sweet musician, holds her slave;
 For whose life I deem it duty
  Death, ev'n death itself to brave.
LY. Me my Calais with such ardour
  Courts and kisses—him to spare—
 Death, or was there aught still harder,
  I ten thousand times would bear.
HO. What if our old flame recover,
  And our hearts again subdue,
 While the portal of your lover,
  Shut to Chloe, opes to you?
LY. Tho' he be as bright as brightness,
  Thou with cork, or with the sea,
 Well compar'd for wrath and lightness,
  I could live and die with thee.

*He advises Lyce to lay aside hardheartedness, and to be mild to him
in his state of submission.*

Far away, where Tanais flows,
 Had you been a Scythian's wife—
Yet to see a man expose,
 At your cruel doors, his life,
To the northern blasts a prey,
Might have fill'd you with dismay.

Hear you not the creeking door,
 How the winds, in ruffian haste,
Make the grove-trees howl and roar
 Round the piles of Attic taste;
And how Jove, with purer air,
Glazes snow that settles there!

To the queen of softer mould
 Cast away ungrateful pride,
Lest you chance to lose your hold,
 When the knot of love's unty'd.
You're not of the Tuscan breed,
Right Penelope indeed.—

Tho' nor bribes nor pray'rs prevail
 On that harden'd breast of thine,
Nor complexion, violet-pale,
 Nor your spouse, who 'midst his wine,
Wounded by the vocal art
Of a minstrel, yields his heart.

Spare, yet spare your suppliant swains,
 Rougher than th'obdurate oak,
Or the snakes, which Moorish plains
 To severer spite provoke—
Constitution cannot last,
Thus to bear the stormy blast.

He requests Mercury to suggest to him such strains as may work upon
the affections of Lyde, chusing for his subject the tale of the Danaids.

O Mercury! for thou instill'd
  The notes of old Amphion sung,
Who with his voice could cities build,
And thou, O shell! compleatly fill'd,
  When sev'n-times sweetly strung;
Nor vocal, nor in vogue of yore,
  Now known in palaces and fanes,
In such inviting accents soar,
As may tempt Lyde to her door,
  Attentive to thy strains.
The tygers, with their woodlands wild,
  You to your train in pow'r compel;
You make the rapid torrents mild,
Th'enormous hell-hound heard, and smil'd,
  You play'd your lute so well.
He smil'd—tho' on his Stygian head
  A hundred twisted snakes are hung,
And steams of pestilential dread,
And matter still with poison fed,
  Flow from his triple tongue.
Ixion too, and Tityos, shew'd
  An irksome glimpse of ghastly joy,
While to your melody renew'd,
No more the Danaids pursu'd
  Their task of vain employ.
Let Lyde hear the rueful tale,
  And punishment at last injoin'd,
How they still ply the sieve-like pail,
Which ever must be fill'd to fail,
  The monsters of their kind.

The destiny that must remain
  For crimes beyond the grave to feel—
Impious! what could be more a stain?
Impious! their bridegrooms all were slain
  By their remorseless steel.
But * one of many was a bride,
  Whose merit grac'd the nuptial flame,
To her false father nobly ly'd,
And left her memory the pride
  Of everlasting fame.
Who bade her youthful spouse "arise—
  "Arise (she said) with my reprieve—
"Lest a long sleep should seal your eyes
"Whence least you fear—my father's spies
  "And sisters too deceive—
"Which, like so many beasts of prey,
  "With younglings in their rav'nous claws,
"Ev'n now, alas! thy brethren slay—
"But I will neither strike nor stay
  "Whom gentlest nature awes.
"With chains me let my father load,
  "Because I chose my spouse to spare,
"And pity on distress bestow'd—
"Or make me settle my abode
  "In sharp Numidian air.
"Convey'd by swiftness and the wind,
  "Begone, my love, in peace begone,
"While Venus and the night are kind—
"But when my monument's design'd,
  "Engrave my tale thereon."

*Hypermnestra.

Neobule, smitten with the love of young Hebrus, leads a life of in-
dolence and sloth.

'Tis wretched in earnest to live like a mope,
 Nor wash down chagrin with sweet wine;
To yield to an uncle all spirit and hope,
 Who rails at your pleasures and mine.
The charms of young Hebrus, and love's flying boy,
 Have stol'n your work-basket away,
And all that fine tap'stry that us'd to employ,
 And give to Minerva the day.
This gay Liparean's a notable knight,
 Bellerophon's self he may seem,
Not beat in the battle, or match'd in the flight,
 When fresh from the cruse and the stream.
The same in each motion's as clean as a cat,
 To hurl at the deer in the park,
Thro' bushes and shrubs the wild-boar can come at,
 And his quickness ne'er misses the mark.

He promises a sacrifice to the fountain, whose pleasantness he highly commends.

Hail, clear as crystal to the eyes,
 Blandusia's fav'rite spring;
O worthy to receive the prize
 Of wine and flow'rs we bring;
To-morrow we shall give thy flood
A kid, whose horns begin to bud,
 And fight and wantonness portend:
In vain—his pranks must be no more—
For shortly with his sacred gore
 He thy cool stream shall blend.
Thee scorching Sirius cannot touch—
 You yield a pleasing shade,
Which for the steers, when work'd too much,
 And wand'ring flock's display'd.
Thou shalt be register'd by fame,
A fountain of illustrious name,
 Whilst I thy useful beauties book;
The oak so happy on the spot,
To overhang thine hollow grot,
 Whence spouts thy pratling brook.

This ode contains the praises of Augustus, on his return from Spain, after having defeated the Cantabrians.

Cæsar (of whom but now 'twas said,
  That, like Amphytrion's son,
He went, at hazard of his head,
To buy a wreath from Spain) is sped,
  And has the battle won.
Let * her come forth, whose faithful heart
  Is center'd in her spouse,
So great in military art,
Having to heav'n perform'd her part,
  In rend'ring of her vows.
And let Octavia too be there,
  And, with neat fillets bound,
The mothers of the Roman fair,
And youths the gods have deign'd to spare,
  In triumph to be crown'd.
O lads and lasses newly bless'd,
  That have your bridegrooms known,
Let not a word be now express'd,
But in such decency is dress'd,
  As modesty may own.

139

This day my festival indeed
 Shall banish care and pain,
Nor will I fear by force to bleed,
But from all trouble shall be freed,
 In Cæsar's peaceful reign.
Perfumes and garlands bring to-day,
 And for a measure call,
Whose date preserves the Marsian fray,
If † Spartacus, in quest of prey,
 Has not secur'd them all.
Quick, with her hair set off with myrrh,
 Let me Neæra see,
And bring her lute along with her;
If that cross porter should demur,
 Come back again to me.
A hoary head dispute abates,
 Though tempted to be sour,
Nor appetite for wrath creates—
I had not borne it, by the fates!
 When Plancus was in pow'r.

*Livia, the wife of Augustus.

†Spartacus, the famous gladiator, who stirred up the servile war.

That now being old, she would set some bounds to her impudence and lasciviousness.

Poor Ibycus his wife,
 At length, methinks, 'tis time
To quit your wicked life,
 And each flagitious crime:
You should the better, sure, behave,
Now you are verging on the grave.
 Sure now you should desist,
  Amidst the brilliant stars,
 To spread a gloomy mist:
  For decency debars
That 'mongst the maidens you should play,
Like Pholoe the young and gay.
 Your daughter, with less shame,
  May rouse up our young rakes,
 While Bacchanalian dame
  Her timbrel she awakes;
The love of Nothus makes her brisk,
Like goat upon the hill to frisk.
 The fair Lucerian fleece
  Not rosy wreathes to twine,
 Nor harps are of a piece
  With such an age as thine;
Nor should an antiquated hag
E'er boast of an exhausted cag.

All things are open to gold; but Horace is content with his lot, by which he remains in a state of happiness.

A tow'r of brass, whose doors were barr'd
With oak, while, howling, upon guard,
　Stood dogs, prepar'd to bite,
Had been sufficient, to be sure,
Imprison'd Danae to secure
　From rakes that prowl by night:
If Jove, and she of ocean born,
Had not Acrisius laugh'd to scorn,
　With all his anxious tribe;
A way they found was fair and free,
When once the god should make his plea,
　Transform'd into a bribe.
Gold through the centinels can pass,
And break through rocks and tow'rs of brass,
　Than thunder-bolts more strong:
That * Argive prophet lost his life,
And was undone, because his wife
　Was bought to do him wrong.
The Macedon of such renown,
With gifts the city-gates broke down,
　And foil'd his rival kings:
Gifts ev'n can naval chiefs ensnare,
Though rough and honest, they would care
　For more superior things.
Anxiety pursues increase,
And craving never like to cease —
　I have myself deny'd
With cause to lift my crest on high,
And with such men as thee to vie,
　O knighthood's peerless pride.
The more a man himself refrains,
The more from hea'vn his virtue gains:
　I pitch my tent with those
Who their desires, like me, divest,
And, as an enemy profest,
　The slaves of wealth oppose.

More noble in my lowly lot,
Than if together I had got
   Whate'er th'Appulian ploughs;
And poor amongst great riches still,
The fruit of no mean toil and skill,
   Could in my garners house.
A wood of moderate extent,
And stream of purest element,
   And harvest-home secure,
Make me more happy than the weight
Of Africa's precarious state
   Of empire could ensure.
What tho' nor sweet Calabrian bee
Makes his nectarious comb for me,
   Nor Formian wine grows old
Within my cellars many a year,
Though from rich Gallic meads I shear
   No fleeces of the fold:
Yet want's remote, that wretched fate,
That makes a man importunate—
   If more I should require,
I should not be refus'd by you—
But I must raise my revenue
   By curbing my desire.
And better so, than should I add
The Lydian realm to what I had,
   And all the Phrygian land;
They that crave most, possess the least—
'Tis well where'er enough's the feast;
   Heav'n gives with frugal hand.

Amphiaraus, a Grecian prophet, foreseeing that he should die at the siege of Troy, kept himself concealed; but was betrayed by his wife, for the sake of a golden necklace.

He extols the nobility of Lamia—He then advises him to spend the morrow with merriment.

O sprung from Lamus! fam'd of old,
Since by our fathers we were told,
That you from him your family derive,
And diaries that feast each rising year revive.
From him, your fountain-head, you spring,
Who was a most extensive king,
And first the Formian walls was said to found
On Liris for Marica in his current bound.
To-morrow's eastern blast shall speed
To strew with leaves and useless weed
The groves, unless th'old raven's voice be vain,
That witch of rising winds, and of descending rain.
On your glad hearth dry billets raise,
And (while 'tis lawful) let 'em blaze;
Indulge to-morrow on fat pig and wine,
And servants call'd from work, with their gay lord to dine.

*The Ælian family was very illustrious in Rome, and very numerous—it comprehended likewise the house of Lamia, which did to it distinguished honour on account of its antiquity, insomuch that, if a man was better born than ordinary, he was proverbially called a Lamia.

He beseeches the sylvan god, that, in traversing his fields, he would be
propitious to Horace and his stock.

O Faunus! ardent to pursue
 The nymphs that from thee bound,
Propitious all my fields review,
My sunny haunts—and favour shew
 To all my younglings round.
If yearly with a tender kid
 Thy presence we invoke,
And if to love and feasting bid,
You daily see th'old altar hid
 In wreathes of fragrant smoke.
The cattle on the grassy plain,
 Disport in active play;
Both men and flocks at ease remain,
December's nones to entertain,
 Which, Faunus, is thy day.
The wolf amongst the lambs is seen,
 And by the sheep's defy'd;
Down falls the foliage ever-green,
The delvers dance with joyous mien,
 And throw their spades aside.

He raillies him in a jocose manner, that, describing ancient histories, he neglects things pertaining to a merry life.

How distant from th'Inachian root
Was patriot * Codrus, who so bravely fell,
You in your histories compute,
Of Peleus' race, and Trojan wars you tell,
But what a cask of Chian costs,
And who the bath shall temper and prepare,
When I shall 'scape these chilling frosts,
And at whose house, to mention you forbear.
Fill up, my boy, for this new moon,
For midnight, and Muræna's num'rous † poll,
Mix liquor handily and soon,
Three or nine bumpers in each toper's bowl.
The bard that loves th'odd-number'd train
Of Muses, takes nine bumpers in his glee.
The grace, with naked sisters twain,
Fearful of wrangling, will admit but three.
It is my pleasure to be mad,
Why cease to blow the Berecynthian horn?
Why hang the pipe and harp so sad?
All niggard hearts and sparing hands I scorn.
Bring roses, bring abundance in,
Let neighbour Lycus, and his blooming girl,
Unfit for Lycus, hear our din,
To mortify that old invidious churl.
At thee, with bushy hair so spruce,
And bright as Vesper, buxom Chloe aims;
Me slow-consuming cares reduce,
As Glycera now checks, now fans the flames.

The last king of Athens, who gave his life for the good of his country. The Lacedemonians being engaged in war with the Athenians, were told by the oracle, that those should get the victory whose general should happen to be slain. Codrus, hearing of this, disguised himself, and went amongst the Lacedemonians, whom he provoked by abuse to put him to death, upon which the Athenians came off victorious.

† *At which Muræna was chosen augur.*

That he should not force away the beautiful Nearchus from his mistress.

O Pyrrhus! what art thou about,
  The lioness's cubs to move,
And take her very fav'rite out?
Full soon the plund'rer, none-so-stout,
  Th'attack will disapprove.
When he shall pass along the train
  Of rakes, that for their mistress stir,
Who shall have best of the campaign,
Shalt thou thy friend to good regain,
  Or leave to vice and her?
Mean time, while you the darts acute
  Present—she whets her dreadful tooth,
Lo! he degrades beneath his foot
That palm, the price of this dispute,
  The long-contested youth,
With his loose locks perfum'd and curl'd,
  For sportive zephyrs there to play,
Like Nireus in his form begirl'd,
Or * who, from Ida and the world,
  To heav'n was snatch'd away.

*Ganymede.

He pleasantly admonishes it to pour out old wine for the sake of Cor-
vinus, from whence he takes occasion to commemorate the praises of
wine in general.

O cask! that bears, like me, thy date
From Manlius his consulate,
Whether with murmurs, jests, or brawlings fraught,
Or mad amours, or sleep, the kind relief of thought!
Whatever be your long intent,
Choice Massic, worthy to have vent
On a good day, come forth at the behest
Of my Corvinus, come with mellowness and zest.
Not he, tho' forward to imbibe
The lore of the Socratic tribe,
Will brutish scorn thee—Cato, as they say,
Would often warm with wine his virtue and his clay.
To lend to sluggish minds a lift—
And brighten harshness is thy gift—
You take the cares from out a wiseman's breast,
And make our politicians with their secrets jest.
You doubtful minds by hope ensure,
The horns exalting of the poor,
Who, after he has fairly drank thee down,
Nor heeds the soldier's arms, nor dreads the tyrant's frown.
Bacchus and Venus on the spot,
And graces ever in a knot,
And living lamps shall eke thee out to-night,
Till Phœbus drive the stars with his superior light.

148

He consecrates the pine, which hangs over his villa, to Diana, whose
offices he celebrates.

Queen of the mountains far and near,
 And of the woodlands wild,
Who, thrice invok'd, art swift to hear,
 And save the maids with child;
This pine, that o'er my villa tow'rs,
And from its eminence embow'rs,
 I dedicate alone to thee;
Where ev'ry year a pig shall bleed,
Lest his obliquity succeed
 Against thy fav'rite tree.

The gods are to be worshipped with clean hands, and conscience of a well-spent life.

If, heav'n-address'd, your hands and knees
At each new moon the gods appease,
And if a pig you slay, my rustic dame,
And offer your first-fruits with incense in the flame;
Your fruitful vineyard then shall scorn
The Afric blast, nor shall your corn
Be scarce or blighted—nor the fatal stroke,
Amidst th'autumnal plenty reach your little folk.
For the vow'd victim, that is fed
Where Algidum his snowy head
'Midst holms and oaks uprears, or in the mead
Of Alba, must beneath the pontiff's hatchet bleed.
If you the lares crown and clean,
With myrtle and with froth marine,
'Tis not requir'd that such as you and I
Should on our altar cause whole hecatombs to die,
If there a spotless hand you place,
A sumptuous victim, in that case,
Will not with heav'n more sure acceptance make,
Than mix'd with good intent the little salted cake.

Though richer than the hoarded gain
Of Araby and Ind unplunder'd yet,
  You of th'Appulian and Tyrrhenian main,
Should with casoons and piers possession get;
  If deepest on the highest head
Dire fate his adamantine hooks will drive,
  You cannot rid your fearful soul from dread,
Nor from the snares of death escape contrive.
  The Scythians have a better lot,
Who dwell in plains, and carry in a cart
  From place to place their customary cot,
And those rough Getans, negligent of art,
  Whose common acres, unsurvey'd,
Yield corn and fruit, that's bread for all the race;
  Nor do they drive the plough, or ply the spade,
Above a year in one continu'd place.
  And when their annual toil is o'er,
Another set the vacant lands receive,
  Who on the self-same terms with those before,
As they succeed, the prior hands relieve.
  There her step-children's orphan life
The woman in her innocence will spare;
  Nor does the man obey a portion'd wife,
Nor does she make a well-dress'd rake her care.
  Their parents' great and virtuous fame,
And, cautious, constant chastity's their dow'r.
  Thus runs the law: "Keep clear of sin and shame,
"Or death's the wages from offended pow'r."
  O that some sage would rise to quell
Our impious slaughter, and our civil rage,
  Fond as his country's father to excel—
So call'd beneath his bust—let him engage
  Our monstrous licence to revise—
Fam'd to the latest times—since we, O shame!

151

Hate virtue, when she's seen before our eyes,
But envious, when she's gone, her worth proclaim.
 For what are all these woful cries,
If sin by punishment is not cut off? —
Laws without morals! — Can mere forms suffice
For any thing but vanity and scoff?
 If such presumption still subsists,
That neither torrid zone, nor northern pole,
 Nor solid snow, that mountain-high exists,
Can terrify the merchant's sordid soul?
 The mariners expertly dare
The horrid seas; for in their rough account
 Want is disgrace — they rather do or bear
All ills, than virtue's arduous way surmount.
 Let us our gold and gems refund,
Source of our woe, into the neighb'ring main,
 Or Capitol, where all our ears are stunn'd,
With party clamours, and the servile train.
 If we are penitent in truth,
The very seeds of vice should be eras'd,
 And the too tender spirits of our youth,
And nerves with exercise severer brac'd.
 Our noble youth have got no seat
Upon their horse, and fear to urge the chace,
 As far more learned in the idle feat
Of Grecian tops, or law-forbidden ACE.
 Mean time the father's perjur'd heart
Imposes on his partner and his guest,
 And hastes to try each method, and each mart,
To make a worthless heir of wealth possest.
 For why? Ill-gotten goods increase —
Yet after all their toil and time mis-spent,
 They have acquir'd by far too much for peace,
And far too little to insure content.

Roused by an inward goad from Bacchus, he proposes to speak cer-
tain new Lyrics concerning Augustus.

Bacchus, with thy spirit fraught,
Whither, whither am I caught?
To what groves and dens am driv'n,
Quick with thought, all fresh from heav'n?
In what grot shall I be found,
While I endless praise resound,
Cæsar to the milky way,
And Jove's synod to convey?
Great and new, as yet unsung
By another's lyre or tongue,
Will I speak—and so behave,
As thy sleepless dames, that rave
With enthusiastic face,
Seeing Hebrus, seeing Thrace,
And, where feet barbarian go,
Rhodope so white with snow.
How I love to lose my way,
And the vastness to survey
Of the rocks and desarts rude,
With astonishment review'd!
O of nymphs, that haunt the stream,
And thy priestesses supreme!
Who, when strengthen'd at thy call,
Can up-tear the ash-trees tall,
Nothing little, nothing low,
Nothing mortal will I show.
'Tis adventure—but 'tis sweet
Still to follow at thy feet,
Wheresoe'er you fix your shrine,
Crown'd with foliage of the vine.

Worn out at length with old age, he takes leave of the lyre and his
love affairs.

Of late an able am'rous swain,
I made full many a great campaign;
But now my harp and arms, of edge bereft,
Shall hang upon this wall, which rising on the left
In sea-born Venus' temple stands —
Here bring the torches and the brands;
Here bring the wrenching-irons and the bows
Against obstructing doors, so big with threats and blows.
Yet, goddess, of rich Cyprus queen,
And Memphis, where no snow is seen,
Once gently, with thy long-extended whip,
Touch my coquettish Chloe, till you make her skip.

He dissuades her especially from the example of Europa.

The screamings of th'ill-omen'd jay,
  Or pregnant bitch, or fox attend,
Or tauny wolf in quest of prey,
All wicked wretches in their way,
    And to their journey's end:
Or let a serpent drive them back,
  The road swift crossing like a dart,
And terrify the stumbling hack—
For thee I dread no such attack;
    But with an augur's art,
In early pray'r I will apply,
  That some good-natur'd crow may speed,
And leave the east before the cry
Of birds that bode a stormy sky,
    And to their lakes proceed.
O Galatea! be thou blest,
  Where'er you choose to take your rout,
And keep my mem'ry in your breast;
Nor raven nor the pye molest
    Your course, as you set out.
But look, as he's in haste to set,
  How prone Orion moves the seas,
I well know Adrian's gloomy threat,
And how much mischief's to be met
    From yonder whit'ning breeze.
May wives and children of our foes
  The rising goat's alarm partake;
To the black surge themselves expose,
Which, roaring to the blast that blows,
    Makes all the land to quake.

Thus did Europa trust, of yore,
  To that false bull her snowy limbs,
And, trembling at her boldness, bore
Her midmost course, where, far from shore,
  Full many a monster swims.
She, who of late the meadows knew,
  Fair student of the flow'ry bloom,
Wove chaplets to the wood-nymphs due—
Nought now but stars and waves could view,
  All in the glimm'ring gloom.
And when she was arriv'd at Crete,
  So famous for its hundred towns,
O father! lost and indiscrete,
The daughter's duty to defeat,
  She cry'd, in wrath, and frowns.
Whence? Whither am I come?—Too light
  A punishment one death would be—
Am I awake, and wail of right?
Or is't a vision of the night,
  And I from baseness free?
A vision from the iv'ry gate,
  Which brings false fancies to the head—
Say, was it then a better fate
Through the long seas to sail—or wait
  Where new-blown flow'rs are spread?
O if I had th'audacious steer
  My indignation hates and scorns,
I'd kill him with a falchion here,
And, though he was of late so dear,
  Would strive to break his horns.

156

Shameless I left my father's place,
  Shameless I wait the doom of hell—
Ye gods! if any hear my case—
O that I naked, in disgrace,
  Might roam 'mongst lions fell!
Before a virulent decay
  Shall feed upon my blooming cheek,
While yet there's moisture in my clay,
To be the tyger's tender prey,
  With all my charms, I seek.
Ah base! thy father to offend,
  Whose passion urges thee to die;
Well did thy girdle thee attend—
Thyself upon this ash suspend,
  And with his will comply.
Or if, upon the rocks to split,
  Acute with death, you are inclin'd;
To the fierce storm yourself submit—
Unless, perhaps, you should think fit
  To ply a task injoin'd,
And live a tyrant's harlot vile,
  And bear his queen's imperious tongue—
Thus, as she urg'd her plaintive stile,
Came Venus with perfidious smile,
  And boy with bow unstrung—
Anon, when she had jeer'd enough,
  She said, forbear your wrath and heat,
Since with his horns, though ne'er so tough,
This bull shall meet a full rebuff,
  When you with him shall treat.
Do you not know your fame and fort,
  As matchless Jove's distinguish'd dame—
Learn your high dignity at court—
And let the quarter'd world support
  Your story and your name.

He exhorts Lyde to pass the day sacred to Neptune merrily, in drinking and singing.

Neptune, on his festal day,
 How can we so well exalt?
Lyde, bring without delay
 Wine from out our inmost vault;
Thus you, with a fresh resource,
Wisdom's fort shall reinforce.

Don't you see the day decline?
 Yet, as if the sun would wait,
You neglect to bring the wine,
 Which is of most pleasant date;
For when * Bibulus was chose,
It was laid to his repose.

We will sing alternate lays—
 Neptune and the Nereids green,
I with lively verse will praise—
 You, Latona, pow'rful queen,
And swift-darting Dian's laud,
With your twisted lyre applaud.

And the end of all to crown,
 We will chant the queen of smiles,
Who with harness'd swans comes down
 Unto all her fav'rite isles;
And as goddess of delight,
We will deify the night.

Bibulus signifies a toper.

He invites him to a chearful supper, omitting public concerns.

O from Tyrrhenian monarchs sprung!
  This many a season I forbear
A cask of mellow wine, untouch'd by tongue,
With roses for thy breast, and essence for thy hair.
  Dispatch—nor Tibur's marshy meads,
    Nor always Esula admire,
  Whose sloping soil the eye with verdure feeds,
Nor buildings rais'd aloft by * him who slew his sire.
  Leave squeamish plenty, and the pile,
    Whose structures to the skies presume,
  And cease to praise in such a pompous style
The smoke, and wealth, and clamour of your prosp'rous Rome.
  'Tis joy, at times, to shift the scene,
    As men of wealth and pow'r allow,
  And without purple carpets neat and clean,
The poor man's cottage-treat has smooth'd an anxious brow.
  Now Cepheus drives his flaming car,
    Now Procyon's wrath begins to burn;
  Now the mad lion shews his rampant star,
As fiery Phœbus makes the drinking-days return.
  Now weary to the stream and shade
    Go shepherds with their languid sheep,
  Or where Sylvanus spreads his thickest glade,
And on the silent bank vague winds are lull'd asleep.
  What regulations best may suit
    The state, and for the world you care,
  What points the Seres, Bactrians would dispute,
And what discordant Tanais rises to prepare.
  Wisely do heav'nly pow'rs th'event
    Of future times in night suppress,
  And smile when mortal men are too intent
Beyond their reach—Take thought, that moment you possess
  To husband—As for other cares,
    As with the streaming river's course
  Now gliding to the Tuscan sea it fares,
Now wave-worn rocks, and trunks up-torn with rapid force,

And flocks and houses in its flood
Involving, not without the roar
Of Echo—mountains and th'adjoining wood,
When deluge boils the streams above the peaceful shore.
He, master of himself, shall dwell,
And in a state of joy subsist,
Who every day his heart can fairly tell—
"Why this is life."—To-morrow with a gloomy mist,
Or brightness Jove may deck the pole,
Yet shall he never take away
The past, or with his utmost pow'r controul
That bliss, the fleeting hours have ravish'd as their prey.
Delighted with her cruel pow'r,
Still trifling insolently blind,
Fortune shifts short-liv'd honours ev'ry hour,
Now good, perhaps, to me, now to another kind.
I praise her while I call her mine;
But if she spread her wings for flight,
Wrapt in my virtue, I her gifts resign,
And court ingenuous want, whose portion is her mite.
'Tis not my business, though the mast
Should with the southern whirlwinds groan,
With wretched pray'rs to deprecate the blast,
Lest in the greedy main my bales be overthrown.
In such a case, my little boat,
For which two oars alone are made,
Should bear me through th'Egean dread afloat,
Fann'd by the gentle breeze, and safe in Castor's aid.

Telegonas.

Horace has gained eternal glory by his lyric compositions.

I've made a monument to pass
The permanence of solid brass,
And rais'd to a sublimer height
Than pyramids of royal state,
Which washing rains, or winds that blow
With vehemence, cannot o'erthrow:
Nor will th'innumerable tale
Of years, or flight of time avail.
For death shall never have the whole
Of Horace, whose immortal soul
Shall 'scape the pow'rs of human bane,
And for new praise his works remain,
As long as priest and silent maid
Shall to the Capitol parade;
Where Aufidus in rapture goes,
And where poor Daunus scarcely flows,
Once rural king—I shall be thought
The prince of Roman bards, that brought
To Italy th'Æolian airs,
Advanc'd from want to great affairs.
Assume, Melpomene, that pride,
Which is to real worth ally'd;
And in good-will descending down,
With Delphic bays my temples crown.

Horace is now arrived to that time of day, when he ought to alienate himself from love affairs, and ludicrous verses.

Left alone so long a season,
  What! again new warfare rage?
Spare me, Venus, treason! treason!
  This is not a lover's age.
Now no more my youthful vigour
  Good queen Cynara inspires—
Cease to use thy gentle rigour,
  Parent fierce of sweet desires.
Staid, and void of inclination—
  Almost fifty—hence depart
To the softer invocation
  Of full many a youthful heart.
On more equable condition
  Drive your purple swans away,
And put Paulus in commission
  At a better time of day.
For he's nobly born, and decent,
  Would you fire a worthy breast?
And great instances are recent,
  How he pleads for the distrest.
Youth of most accomplish'd merit,
  Of an hundred arts and charms—
He shall bear with strength and spirit
  Far and wide thy conqu'ring arms.
If he smile at times prevailing
  O'er a bribing dupe's disgrace,
With sweet wood thy bust empaling,
  He near Alba's lake shall place.
Thine indulgent presence thither
  Shall much frankincense invite,
Lyre, and flute, and pipe together
  Shall thy ravish'd ears delight.
Twice a day the lads and lasses
  There thy praises shall resound,
And with foot that snow surpasses,
  Salian-like, shall shake the ground.

163

It is hazardous to imitate the ancient poets.

Whoever vies with Pindar's strain,
  With waxen wings, my friend, would fly,
Like him who nam'd the glassy main,
    But could not reach the sky.
Cascading from the mountain's height,
  As falls the river swoln with show'rs,
Deep, fierce, and out of measure great
    His verses Pindar pours.
Worthy to claim Apollo's bays,
  Whether his dithyrambics roll,
Daring their new-invented phrase
    And words, that scorn controul.
Or gods he chants, or kings, the seed
  Of gods, who rose to virtuous fame,
And justly Centaurs doom'd to bleed,
    Or quench'd Chimera's flame.
Or champions of th'Elean justs,
  The wrestler, charioteer records,
And, better than a hundred busts,
    He gives divine rewards.
Snatch'd from his weeping bride, the youth
  His verse deplores, and will display
Strength, courage, and his golden truth,
    And grudges death his prey.
The Theban swan ascends with haste,
  Of heav'n's superior regions free;
But, I, exactly in the taste
    Of some Matinian bee,
That hardly gets the thymy spoil
  About moist Tibur's flow'ry ways,
Of small account, with tedious toil,
    Compose my labour'd lays.

You, bard indeed! with more applause
 Shall Cæsar sing, so justly crown'd,
As up the sacred hill he draws
    The fierce Sicambrians bound.
A greater and a better gift
 Than him, from heav'n we do not hold,
Nor shall—although the times should shift
    Into their pristine gold.
The festal days and public sports
 For our brave chief's returning here,
You shall recite, and all the courts
    Of law contentions clear.
Then would I speak to ears like thine,
 With no small portion of my voice,
O glorious day! O most divine!
    Which Cæsar bids rejoice.
And while you in procession hie,
 Hail triumph! triumph! will we shout
All Rome—and our good gods supply
    With frankincense devout!
Thee bulls and heifers ten suffice—
 Me a calf weaned from the cow,
At large who many a gambol tries,
    Though doom'd to pay my vow.
Like the new moon, upon his crest
 He wears a semicircle bright,
His body yellow all the rest,
    Except this spot of white.

Horace was born for poetry, to which his immortality is intirely owing.

He, on whose natal hour you glance
 A single smile with partial eyes,
Melpomene, shall not advance
 A champion for th'Olympic prize,
Nor drawn by steeds of manag'd pride,
In Grecian car victorious ride.

Nor honour'd with the Delphic leaf,
 A wreath for high atchievements wove,
Shall he be shewn triumphant chief,
 Where stands the Capitol of Jove,
As justly rais'd to such renown
For bringing boastful tyrants down.

But pleasing streams, that flow before
 Fair Tibur's flow'ry-fertile land,
And bow'ring trees upon the shore,
 Which in such seemly order stand,
Shall form on that Eolic plan
The bard, and magnify the man.

The world's metropolis has deign'd
 To place me with her darling care,
Rome has my dignity maintain'd
 Amongst her bards my bays to wear;
And hence it is against my verse
The tooth of envy's not so fierce.

O mistress of the golden shell!
 Whose silence you command, or break;
Thou that canst make the mute excel,
 And ev'n the sea-born reptiles speak;
And, like the swan, if you apply
Your touch, in charming accents die.

This is thy gift, and only thine,
 That, as I pass along, I hear—
"There goes the bard, whose sweet design
 "Made lyricks for the Roman ear."
If life or joy I hold or give,
By thee I please, by thee I live.

As him, by mighty Jove preferr'd
  On high his thunder-bolts to bear,
Deem'd o'er the winged race the sovereign bird,
E'er since he made sweet youth, and innocence his care;
  Of old, green years, but strength innate,
    Drove him, unskill'd, upon his prey,
And vernal winds, the winter out of date,
Taught him unwonted flights, but not without dismay,
  Anon, by vivid impulse sped,
    He wages war against the folds,
And by his lust of fight and plunder led,
The curv'd-reluctant snakes within his claws he holds.
  Or as a goat in pastures green
    Intent, a lion's tawny whelp
(Whom his fierce mother did but lately wean)
Eyes rushing with new fangs, and has no hope of help.
  Such warrior Drusus in his bloom
    The Rhœtian and North-Alpine band
Beheld (which latter whence they did assume
With Amazonian ax long since to arm their hand,
  I have omitted to declare,
    Nor can we every matter know)
But far and wide victorious as they were,
The young man's wondrous conduct taught them at a blow,
  How a well-bent ingenuous mind,
    And genius disciplin'd can awe,
Whose plan was in a happy school design'd
By Cæsar, more than father to his sons-in-law.
  The brave are gender'd by the brave,
    This truth ev'n genuine steers attest,
The manag'd steeds by progeny behave,
Nor are tame turtles hatch'd in yon fierce eagle's nest.
  Yet learning inward strength assists,
    And education mans the heart;
Refinement by morality exists,
Or else good-nature fails for want of wholesome art.
  What to the Neroes Rome should pay,
    The loud Metaurus witness bears,
And vanquish'd Asdrubal—and that fair day
Which clear'd the low'ring gloom from our distress'd affairs.

That day, which many a prize renowns,
  First mention'd victory to gain,
When Hannibal fled thro' th'Italian towns,
Like wind that sweeps the sea, or fire that takes the train.
  From this desirable event
    The Roman enterprizes throve,
And ravag'd, where the Punic plund'rers went,
The temples stood repair'd in every sacred grove;
  Until the traitor said at last,
    "Like stags, of rav'nous wolves the prey,
"We follow those heroic bands too fast,
"Of whom by craft and flight we solely win the day.
  "The nation, which from Troy on fire,
    "Held sacred from their numerous woes,
"Brought through the Tuscan seas the son and sire,
"In fair Ausonia's towns from shipwreck to repose,
  "As from the ax the hardy oak,
    "Which in dark Algidus abounds,
"Tho' hurt and damag'd by the frequent stroke,
"Thrives, and exalts his head, aspiring by its wounds:
  "Not more increase did Hydra, maim'd,
    "Against griev'd Hercules assume,
"Nor was or Thebes, nor was ev'n Colchis, fam'd
"For prodigies, more great, more wonderful than Rome.
  "Sunk to the center, they will rise
    "More fair, and woe to him that strives;
"From vet'ran victors they will win the prize,
"And send the gallant tale to entertain their wives.
  "No more my proud couriers I send
    "To Carthage fall'n, ah fall'n! and fled
"Is all our hope; nor fortune is our friend
"(Though once she lov'd our name) now Asdrubal is dead."
  Nothing so glorious in the field,
    But Claudius will with ease atchieve;
Whom Jove defends, with prudence for his shield,
Thro' intricate distress and war his way to cleave.

That he would at length return to Rome.

From gods propitious sprung, O guard
Of Roman greatness! you retard
  Now far too long your stay:
That promise of a quick return
You made the HOUSE, no more adjourn,
  But keep a shorter day.
Restore to this thy native place
The light, good chief, for when thy face,
  Like spring, its lustre throws,
The day goes off with more content,
And in a better firmament
  A brighter sunshine glows.
As for her son a mother's pain'd,
Above the destin'd year detain'd,
  By southern blasts malign,
Beyond Carpathian waves profound,
Where he continues weather-bound,
  For his sweet home to pine.
With calculations, tears, and sighs,
And vows, she calls, nor turns her eyes
  From off the winding shore;
Ev'n with that fondness these desires
Cæsar his native land requires,
  Still wanted more and more.
For where you are, the grazing steer
Roams o'er the meadows, free from fear,
  Ceres yields ampler fruit;
The sailors plow the peaceful main,
And honour, cautious of a stain,

Keeps accusation mute.
Each house is clear of guilt impure,
Example and the laws secure
 The heart from filthy sin;
For penalty sticks close to blame;
Our ladies are of peerless fame
 For children like their kin.
The Parthian, or with ice congeal'd
Who fears the Scythian in the field,
 Or who the monstrous host
That Germany brings forth and sends,
Or who the threats from Spain attends,
 While Cæsar keeps his post?
Each Roman sends the sun to bed
On his own hill, and loves to wed
 To widow'd elms the vine,
Thence home at night he goes alert,
And thee, as god of his desert,
 Invites to grace his wine.
Thee their incessant pray'rs adore,
And large libations on the floor,
 Are offer'd to thy state;
Thou with the houshold-gods art join'd,
As Greece her Castor bore in mind,
 And Hercules the great.
Long may'st thou give, O glorious chief!
To Rome this leisure and relief,
 So constant patriots pray;
Thus sober in the morn we cry,
Thus in the night with bumpers high,
 When ocean hides the day.

God, whose dread power the * Theban queen
 Felt for her boastings proud and vain,
And Tityos ravisher obscene,
And Peleus' son, who might have been
    High Ilion's fatal bane;
The soldier, braver than them all,
 No match for thee was taught to fear,
Though him her child did Thetis call,
And though he shook the Dardan wall,
    Arm'd with tremendous spear.
As falls to biting steel the pine,
 Or Cypress to the eastern gust,
So he was humbled to resign
His life, extended, and recline
    His neck in Trojan dust.
He in no wooden horse disguis'd,
 For sacred rites of false report,
The Trojan dupes would have surpris'd,
'Midst feasts and dances ill-advis'd,
    In city and at court.
But boldly fierce, with open ire,
 Alas! alas! the dreadful doom
Had gratify'd his vengeance dire,
And infants burnt with Grecian fire,
    Ev'n in their mother's womb.
If not by thee wrought to relent,
 And Venus in persuasion skill'd,
The sire of gods had giv'n assent
That for more fortunate event,
    Æneas walls should build.

O lyrist, with a master's air,
 By whom the sweet Thalia plays,
Which in cool Xanthus lav'st thy hair,
Make thou the Daunian muse thy care,
  Enlightner of our ways.
Phœbus, my spirit, taste, and flame,
 Gives all the gifts that verse adorn;
From him I have the poet's name—
"Ye virgins of unspotted fame,
 "And youths most nobly born,
"Wards of the Delian maid, so fleet
 "'Gainst stags and ounces with her bow,
"Take notice of the Lesbian feet,
"And, as the time you see me beat,
  "Attend to fast and slow,
"Extolling with the ritual praise
 "Latona's darling in your song,
"And her that nightly mends her blaze,
"As shedding her fructiferous rays,
  "She rolls the months along.
"Soon when you're marry'd each shall say,
 "I too was present to rehearse,
"Upon that memorable day,
"The numbers of th'Horatian lay,
  "Skill'd in his mystic verse."

*Niobe.

All things are changed by time; one ought therefore to live chearfully.

The melted snow the verdure now restores,
   And leaves adorn the trees;
The season shifts—subsiding to their shores
   The rivers flow with ease.
The Grace, with nymphs and with her sisters twain,
   Tho' naked dares the dance—
That here's no permanence the years explain,
   And days, as they advance.
The air grows mild with zephyrs, as the spring
   To summer cedes the sway,
Which flies when autumn hastes his fruits to bring,
   Then winter comes in play.
The moons their heav'nly damages supply—
   Not so the mortal star—
Where good Eneas, Tullus, Ancus lie,
   Ashes and dust we are.
Who knows if heav'n will give to-morrow's boon
   To this our daily pray'r?
The goods you take to keep your soul in tune,
   Shall scape your greedy heir.
When you shall die, tho' Minos must acquit
   A part so nobly play'd;
Race, eloquence, and goodness, from the pit
   Cannot restore your shade.
For nor Diana's heav'nly pow'r or love,
   Hippolytus revives;
Nor Theseus can Perithous remove
   From his Lethean gives.

173

There is nothing that can immortalize rather than the works of poets.

Goblets to every friend of gold,
And statues of Corinthian mould,
In gratitude I had bestow'd,
Attending to the present mode;
And tripods too, which were the mead,
That Greece her valiant sons decreed;
Nor shou'd you have the meanest prize,
Were I enrich'd with such supplies,
As Scopas or Parrhasius send,
The one his colours skill'd to blend;
The one, whose excellence is known
To cut a god or man in stone:
But I keep no toy-treasures hid,
Nor do you want them if I did:
Your taste is of a nobler flight,
And poetry is your delight;
Which I can furnish, and assign
The merit of the gift divine.

Not marbles, that the public place
With long inscriptions on the base,
By which returns beyond the grave
New life and spirit to the brave;
Not Hannibal what time he fled,
With threats retorted on his head;
Not impious Carthage, all a-flame,
To greater brightness raise his name,
(Who, when from conquests he return'd,
The title AFRICANUS earn'd)
Than he, who those achievements sung,
Ev'n Ennius from Calabria sprung;
Nor, if our writings shou'd be mute,
Wou'd benefit receive its fruit.

What wou'd the acts of him the son
Of Mars, and what had Ilia done;
If silence, envious of renown,
Had borne their matchless merits down?
The virtue, votes, and pow'rful word
Of bards, have Eacus transferr'd
From Stygian darkness, to the isles
Where happiness eternal smiles.
The muse excepts against the doom
Of meritorious men in Rome.
The muse can bless you to the skies—
'Twas thus brave Hercules cou'd rise
To taste with Jove, a welcome guest,
Celestial fare amongst the rest.
'Tis thus the fam'd twin-stars obtain,
To save ships shatter'd on the main;
Thus, ivy-crown'd, the god of wine
Gives furth'rance to each fair design.

The writings of Horace will never be lost: virtue, without verse, is liable to oblivion. He will sing the praises of Lollius, whose particular excellencies he likewise commemorates.

Lest you should think the strains will die,
　Which I in skill but newly found
With voice to correspondent strings ally,
Borne where from far the rocks of Aufidus resound.
　Know, that if Homer take the lead,
　　Yet is not Pindar out of date;
　Nor Cean nor Alcean fire recede,
Nor that * Sicilian bard's authority and weight.
　Nor if of old Anacreon sung,
　　Has time his sportive lays suppress'd;
　Alive are all the notes of Sappho's tongue,
Which to her lyre she play'd, of genuine warmth possess'd.
　Helen was not the only fair,
　　That was enamour'd to admire
Th' adult'rer's golden garb, and flowing hair,
And royal equipage, with all their grand attire.
　Nor Teucer, from Cydonian string,
　　Was first that with his darts engag'd;
　Nor Troy but once besieged, nor Cretan king,
Nor Sthenelus alone the well-sung contest wag'd.
　Not Hector, val'rous as he was,
　　Nor fierce Deiphobus begun
　To bleed and suffer in their country's cause,
Or for a virtuous wife, or for a darling son.

Before great Agamemnon shone,
  Heroes there were—but all in night,
 Long night, are buried, piteous and unknown,
For want of sacred bards their glories to recite.
  Virtue conceal'd is next, I deem,
  To bury'd sloth—I will not spare
 For ornament, when Lollius is the theme;
Nor suffer so much merit, such a life of care
  In black oblivion to be hurl'd—
  You, Lollius, have a noble mind;
 Skilful and fraught with knowledge of the world,
Equal for all events, or temp'rate or resign'd.
  Of greedy fraud the judge severe,
  Forbearing all-attractive gold;
 A consul not elected for a year,
But still esteem'd, in fact, that dignity to hold,
  Where'er the magistrate prefers
  Things honest to his private ends,
 And bribing villains with a look deters,
And draws against the crowd, and his fair fame defends.
  He is not happy, rightly nam'd,
  Whom large possessions still increase—
 By him more truly is that title claim'd,
Who holds the gifts divine in prudence and in peace;
  Who's able hardship to sustain,
  And dreads vile actions worse than death;
 He for his friends counts any loss a gain,
And for his country's cause will give his dying breath.

Stesichorus.

177

He invites her to a banquet, upon the birth-day of Mæcenas.

Full nine years old my cellar stows
　A cask of good Albanian wine,
And parsley in my garden grows;
For Phyllis chaplets to compose,
　Much ivy too is mine:

With whose green gloss you shall be crown'd;
　With burnish'd plate the house looks gay,
The altar, with chaste vervains bound,
Craves to be * sprinkled from the wound,
　As we the lambkin slay.

All hands are busied—here and there
　Mixt with the lads the lasses fly,
The bustling flames, to dress the fare,
Roll up thick smoke, which clouds the air
　Above the roof on high.

But would you know what joy resides
　With me, to tempt you at this time—
You are to celebrate the ides,
The day which April's month divides,
　And Venus calls her prime;

A feast observable of right,
　Which I more heartily revere,
Than that which brought myself to light,
From whence my patron to requite,
　Flow many a happy year!

Young Telephus, at whom you aim,
　Is not for such as thee at all;
A rich and a lascivious dame
Upon his love has fixt her claim,
　And holds him in sweet thrall.

Let blasted Phaeton dissuade
  Presumptuous hope too high to soar;
And † he a dread example made
By Pegasus, who scornful neigh'd
  That he a mortal bore.

Things worthy of yourself pursue,
  Nor go where vain desire allures;
'Tis lawless to extend your view
To one that's not a match for you—
  Hail! crown of my amours!

For, after this, I will be free
  From every other flame and fair—
Come, learn the song I made for thee,
And join, with charming voice and me,
  To banish gloomy care.

Horace's was a very old altar, so that avet *and the obsolete infinitive* spargier, *are peculiarly happy.*

† *Bellerophon.*

He describes the approach of spring, and invites Virgil to an entertain-
ment upon a certain condition.

Now the breezes fresh from Thrace,
    Those attendants on the spring,
Still the sea, yet urge the race
    Of the ships upon the wing:
No more the meadow's lands are froze,
Nor roar the streams o'ercharg'd with snows.

Now the bird with mournful scream,
    Aye for Itys wont to pine,
Builds her nest, disgrace extreme
    Of the great Cecropian line
E'er since, that most horrid treat
She forc'd the lustful king to eat.

Swains the thriving sheep that tend,
    Thrown upon the mossy sod;
With the pipe their verses blend,
    To divert the rural god:
Whom that sweet scene of flocks and hills,
In Arcady, with rapture fills.

'Tis the time of drinking hard,
    But Calenean would you take,
You must bring a box of nard,
    For your entertainment's sake:
No less can wealthy Virgil frank,
As tutor to our youths of rank.

E'en an ounce of that perfume,
  Shall a special cask intice;
Which in the Sulpician room
  Now sleeps clear of noise and vice:
Fraught with new hopes of cleansing pow'r,
Against the bitter and the sour.

To these pleasures if you haste,
  You must enter with your fee;
You shall not my goblets taste,
  By my inclination, free:
As in the rich man's house you fare,
Without contributing your share.

But, my Virgil, lay aside
  All delay and thirst of gain;
While 'tis lawful to provide,
  'Gainst the seats of death and pain:
Let mirth relieve each grave concern,
For folly's pleasant in its turn.

Book IV. UPON LYCE, AN ANTIQUATED COURTEZAN. Ode XII.

He insults her with extreme bitterness; that now being old, and yet retaining her lustful appetite, she is contemned by the young gallants.

Lyce, the gods my vows have heard,
  At length they've heard my vows;
You wou'd be beauteous with a beard,
  You romp and you carouse:
And drunk, with trembling voice, you court
  Slow Cupid, prone to seek
For better music, bloom, and sport,
  In buxom Chia's cheek.
For he, a sauce-box, scorns dry chips,
  And teeth decay'd and green;
Where wrinkled forehead, and chapt lips,
  And snowy hairs are seen.
Nor Coan elegance, nor gems,
  Your past years will restore;
Which time to his records condemns,
  With fleeting wings of yore.
Ah! where's that form, complexion, grace,
  That air—where is she, say,
That cou'd my sick'ning soul solace,
  And stole my heart away?
Blest! who cou'd Cynara succeed,
  As artful and as fair—
But fate, to Cynara, decreed
  Few summers for her share,
That crow-like Lyce might survive,
  'Till lads shou'd laugh and shout,
To see the torch, but just alive,
  So slowly stinking out.

*Honours, adequate to the merits of Augustus, cannot be attributed by
the Roman Senate and people.*

What can the conscript fathers do,
  Or Romans join'd, with all their souls;
To give th'Augustan worth the honours due,
Grav'd on eternal brass, or written in the rolls.
  O thou, the most illustrious prince,
    Wheree'r the sun the world illumes;
  'Twas thine the rough north Alpines to convince,
What dignity of rank your martial fame assumes.
  For by your troops did Drusus rout
    The fierce Genaunians, Brennians keen
  And, more than once, raz'd many a strong redoubt
They pil'd upon the Alps tremendous to be seen.
  Anon, the elder Nero fought
    A dreadful fight with your success;
  And drove th'enormous Rhetians, quick as thought,
From ev'ry post of war they ventur'd to possess.
  Nero, a glorious sight to see,
    How he bore down the mighty bane
  Of souls, resolv'd to die or to be free,
Ev'n as the south attacks the ocean's proud disdain,
  While Pleiad, and her sisters, cleave
    The clouds, the furious victor sped
  Thro' midmost fire, the murm'ring troops to grieve,
And with his warrior horse ev'n there the troops to head.

As Aufidus, that rolls before
  Appulian Daunus, is in scorn;
And, like the meadow's lord, augments his roar,
And meditates vastation to the fields of corn.
  Thus Claudius, thro' each iron rank
  Of these barbarians, forc'd renown;
And, charging first and hindmost, front and flank,
Victorious, without loss, he mow'd their armies down.
  With thine advice, and prosp'rous fates—
  For, on that memorable day,
When suppliant Alexandria ope'd her gates,
With nought within her courts but terror and dismay.
  Before the fifteen years ran out,
  Fortune successful in the end
The glory, so long wish'd for, brought about,
And made th'imperial arms their final pow'r extend.
  Cantabrians, unsubdu'd till now,
  Medes, Indians, with submissive mien;
Thee the vague Scythian honour and allow,
Guard of the Latian name, and Rome the world's great queen.
  Thee Nilus, that conceals his fount,
  Thee Danube, rapid Tigris fear;
Thee the swoln waves, on which such monsters mount,
'Till British cliffs, remote, the horrid bellowing hear.
  The region of th'intrepid Gaul,
  And all Iberia's harden'd race;
And thee, their lord, the tam'd Sicambrians call,
And, bloody, as they were, thy terms of peace embrace.

Willing to sing upon my lyre,
  The fights we dare, the tow'rs we scale;
Apollo bade me check my fond desire,
Nor on the vast Tyrrhenian spread my little sail.
  Cæsar, in this thy better age,
  Again the fertile fields have throve;
And from proud Parthia's fanes thy godlike rage,
Our standards has retook, and giv'n to Roman Jove.
  And Janus' temple too is clos'd,
  Good order from the peace deriv'd;
And curbs upon licentiousness impos'd,
Have banish'd vice afar, and ancient arts reviv'd.
  From which the Latin name and strength
  Of Italy are so increast,
And our imperial glory, breadth and length,
From the sun's western bed have reach'd remotest east.
  While Cæsar the dominion claims,
  Nor civil rage nor active spite,
Can take us from our peace; nor wrath, whose flames
Forge hostile sounds, and states in friendship disunite.
  Not those that in deep Danube lave,
  Shall now the Julian edicts scorn;
Nor Getans, Seres, or the treach'rous slave
Of Persia, nor the folk upon the Tanais born.
  And we on work and festal days,
  Amidst our cups of jovial wine;
'With wives and children (first with pray'r and praise,
Having made application to the pow'rs divine)
  Will, like our sires, in songs of joy,
  With many a Lydian air between,
Sing our accepted chiefs, Anchises, Troy,
And those descendant heirs of love's indulgent queen.

www.ingramcontent.com/pod-product-compliance
Lightning Source LLC
Chambersburg PA
CBHW061324200626
46813CB00017B/2924